RolePlay

A Comedy

Alan Ayckbourn

A SAMUEL FRENCH ACTING EDITION

SAMUEL
FRENCH
FOUNDED 1830

SAMUELFRENCH-LONDON.CO.UK
SAMUELFRENCH.COM

ISBN 978-0-573-11569-1

www.samuelfrench-london.co.uk

www.samuelfrench.com

FOR AMATEUR PRODUCTION ENQUIRIES

UNITED KINGDOM AND WORLD
EXCLUDING NORTH AMERICA

plays@SamuelFrench-London.co.uk

020 7255 4302/01

Each title is subject to availability from Samuel French,

depending upon country of performance.

Damsels in Distress is a trilogy of plays first seen at the Stephen Joseph Theatre, Scarborough and later at the Duchess Theatre, London. Each of the three comedies is self-contained, the common theme linking them is that the setting for each is the same London Docklands apartment and all three concern young women in various states of distress.

ROLEPLAY

First performed at the Stephen Joseph Theatre, Scarborough, on 4th September 2001. The same production was subsequently presented by Michael Codron, Lee Dean, Michael Linnit, David Ian for ClearChannel Entertainment and Andrew Lloyd Webber, at the Duchess Theatre, London, on 7th September 2002. The cast was as follows:

Julie-Ann Jobson	Saskia Butler
Justin Lazenby	Bill Champion
Paige Petite	Alison Pargeter
Micky Rale	Tim Faraday
Derek Jobson	Robert Austin
Dee Jobson	Beth Tuckey
Arabella Lazenby	Jacqueline King

Directed by Alan Ayckbourn
Designed by Roger Glossop
Lighting design by Mick Hughes
Costume design by Christine Wall

CHARACTERS

Justin Lazenby, 30
Julie-Ann Jobson, his fiancée, 23
Paige Petite, an ex-dancer, 29
Micky Rale, an ex-boxer, 40
Derek Jobson, Julie-Ann's father, 50s
Dee Jobson, Julie-Ann's mother, 45
Arabella Lazenby, Justin's mother, 50s

The action of the play takes place in a riverside apartment
in London's Docklands

SYNOPSIS OF SCENES

ACT I

SCENE 1   Justin's riverside apartment. March. 6pm
SCENE 2   The same—A few minutes later

ACT II   The same—Two hours later

Time: one evening in March

Plays by Alan Ayckbourn published by Samuel French Ltd

Absent Friends
Absurd Person Singular
Bedroom Farce
Body Language
Callisto 5
The Champion of Paribanou
A Chorus of Disapproval
Communicating Doors
Confusions
A Cut in the Rates
Dreams from a Summer House (with John Pattison)
Ernie's Incredible Illucinations
Family Circles
Gizmo
Henceforward...
House & Garden
How the Other Half Loves
Intimate Exchanges (Volume 1 and Volume 2)
It Could Be Any One of Us
Joking Apart
Just Between Ourselves
Living Together
Man of the Moment
Mixed Doubles (*with other authors*)
Mr A's Amazing Maze Plays
Mr Whatnot
My Very Own Story
The Norman Conquests
Relatively Speaking
The Revengers' Comedies
Round and Round the Garden
Season's Greetings
Sisterly Feelings
A Small Family Business
Snake in the Grass
Suburban Strains (with Paul Todd)
Table Manners
Taking Steps
Ten Times Table
Things We Do For Love
This is Where We Came In
Time and Time Again
Time of My Life
Tons of Money (*revisor*)
Way Upstream
Wildest Dreams
Wolf at the Door (*adapter*)
Woman in Mind
A Word from Our Sponsor (with John Pattison)

ACT I

SCENE 1

Justin's riverside apartment on the Thames, somewhere in London's Docklands

A main sitting area and an adjoining walkthrough kitchen/dining area. Sliding windows at one end of the sitting area lead on to a small riverside balcony. At the other end of this sitting area, a well-stocked bar. Near the window, a desk and chair. A sofa, an armchair and a heavy coffee table. A few quite healthy pot plants dotted around. Off this area is a short hallway leading directly to the front door. Also two archways leading to another area visible to us, the common kitchen/dining space. The kitchen end is tidy and well equipped, evidently regularly cleaned. The other end has a small table with two chairs. Leading from this is a further door to the offstage rooms: bedroom, bathroom and a second spare bedroom, usually Justin's study but tonight converted into a dining room

It is six p.m. on a grey, windy March evening. Outside it is raining heavily. We hear the rain occasionally lashing the windows as the wind gusts

Julie-Ann, a woman in her twenties, is in the kitchen area in the process of carefully folding six linen table napkins which she is then placing on to a large tray. She is dressed casually. A particularly loud gust of wind and rain causes her to look anxiously towards the window

Julie-Ann (*calling off*) Hark at it!
Justin (*off, inaudibly*) Hot-hoo-hay?
Julie-Ann (*calling*) Just hark at it!
Justin (*off, inaudibly*) Hwaymin!
Julie-Ann (*calling*) It's getting worse. There's great waves on the river out
    there.
Justin (*off, inaudibly*) Harnteeruyulee.
Julie-Ann (*calling*) Terrible. It's more like the North Sea than the Thames.

Justin, a man of about thirty, appears in the doorway. He is slightly hot and breathless from his exertions

Justin Sorry, Julie? What did you say?

Julie-Ann This weather. Hark at it...

Justin Oh. Yes.

Julie-Ann Hope it doesn't make them late. If it's like this on the motorway...

Justin Well. It may not be.

Julie-Ann I mean, they're coming from Doncaster. If it's like this on the M1...

Justin (*looking out of the window*) Yes, it is rough out there, isn't it? Don't often see it as bad as this.

Julie-Ann I mean, if they break down or have a puncture...

Justin They'll be fine.

Julie-Ann I mean, they're both getting on, you know. And Daddy's never been a very good driver. He likes to turn round to talk to you when he's driving.

Justin Well, he's only bringing your mother, isn't he?

Julie-Ann What's that got to do with it?

Justin Well, won't she be in the front?

Julie-Ann Oh, yes.

Justin Unless they pick up a hitch-hiker.

Julie-Ann finishes her napkin folding

Julie-Ann Oh, no, they never do that. Daddy doesn't approve of them. (*She shows the napkins*) There! What do you think, Justy?

Justin (*frowning a little*) Lovely.

Julie-Ann I'll give you a hand to move that table now, shall I?

Justin No need, I've done it. Wasn't heavy.

Julie-Ann You haven't moved all your stuff as well?

Justin I put it in the bedroom.

Julie-Ann The printer?

Justin Yes.

Julie-Ann And the big computer?

Justin And the scanner. And the speakers, the zip drive. And the mains lead.

Julie-Ann (*kissing him lightly*) Clever darling. Where'd you put it all?

Justin In the bedroom.

Julie-Ann Well done. (*She takes the tray*) Does it work all right in there with the table in the middle?

Justin Just about. Have a look. See what you think.

Julie-Ann goes off with the tray

I think we can just about squeeze six of us round. If we all hold our breath and nobody eats too much.

Julie-Ann (*off, inaudibly*) Hot?
Justin I said—— (*He gives up, calling*) Doesn't matter.
Julie-Ann (*off, inaudibly*) Harnteeru!
Justin (*calling*) Nothing.
Julie-Ann (*off, inaudibly*) Oh, steel get ordimadus found, farthing.
Justin (*calling*) What?
Julie-Ann (*off, inaudibly*) Ormibustle rust slit. Eyes un bosey.
Justin (*only mildly irritated, half to himself*) I can't hear you, Julie!

Justin goes off after her

(*Calling*) What did you say, darling?

The sound of their voices off. We now can't hear either of them

Julie-Ann (*off, inaudibly*) Oh queasily, steel cabbage.
Justin (*off, inaudibly*) Slee pud rye it motherway.
Julie-Ann (*off, inaudibly*) Ho dough weed. Sleall queez bound.
Justin (*off, inaudibly*) Ho hay. Lo hubble.

Julie-Ann enters from the dining room with the empty tray

Julie-Ann (*entering*) No, it's fine, darling, it's perfect where it is. Clever you. We'll all fit round. None of us are that big, are we?

Justin follows her back on

During the following, Julie-Ann starts taking cutlery from a drawer and placing it in neat piles on to the tray. Six of everything plus a number of serving spoons and forks

Justin Sorry, what did you say?
Julie-Ann Your mother's not big, is she?
Justin My mother? No, my mother's ... a normal sort of size.
Julie-Ann Tall?
Justin Yes, she's tall-ish.
Julie-Ann She always is in the photos. Tall's not a problem. (*She thinks for a second*) My father will be fine up that end by the window. He'll be all right there. Not too squashed.
Justin Is your father—well built, then?
Julie-Ann Daddy's—he's quite well built, yes. You know.
Justin Right.
Julie-Ann But then he is very nearly sixty, Justy.

Justin (*a little mystified*) Right.

Slight pause

Julie-Ann (*laughing*) Good job my sister's not coming. She's enormous.
Justin Lucy-Jane?
Julie-Ann No. Not Lucy-Jane. Sally-Jo.
Justin Right. I still get them muddled. Sorry.
Julie-Ann I told you, Lucy-Jane's the one in Canada. The one we don't talk about.
Justin Right.
Julie-Ann Don't for heaven's sake mention her in front of my parents, will you?
Justin I won't.
Julie-Ann You can talk about Sally-Jo all you like.
Justin On the whole, it's probably safer if I don't talk about either of them.
Julie-Ann Just as you like. (*Rather coyly*) You'll have to, though, sooner or later, won't you, darling?
Justin How do you mean?
Julie-Ann Well, when they're both, you know—your sisters-in-law.
Justin Oh, sure. Yes, well... Then. Sure. Yes.
Julie-Ann (*examining the cutlery carefully*) Some of these are filthy, Justy.
Justin Oh, are they?
Julie-Ann Which of us washed up last, I wonder?
Justin No idea...
Julie-Ann I bet it was. You're supposed to wash them properly in hot soapy water, rinse them and then dry them. Not just run them under the tap.
Justin Damn! I must have been off school that day.
Julie-Ann What we really need is a proper dishwasher.
Justin I'll try and find someone. There'll need to be a height restriction, though. They'll have to live under the sink.
Julie-Ann (*oblivious*) It could fit just there perfectly. I mean, once we're—married—we'll be giving dinner parties all the time, won't we?
Justin Once we've got the ballroom open.
Julie-Ann Ballroom? How do you—? (*She realizes he's joking, at last*) Oh! You! Honestly, Justy. You're so naughty sometimes, aren't you?

Justin smiles

(*Blowing a kiss at him*) Always teasing me, aren't you? (*She smiles at him. She turns her attention back to washing the forks. As she does so she sings discordantly*)

Justin winces but tolerates it for a while. Then:

Justin What else do you want me to do?

Julie-Ann (*indicating the kitchen chairs*) You can take those chairs through
   if you like.

Justin Sure.

Julie-Ann We'll keep those two for us. Put those by our places.

Justin Right. How are we all sitting again?

Julie-Ann Justy! How many more times! Daddy at the end...

Justin By the window?

Julie-Ann Correct. Then on his right, me, and then your mother's—man
   friend—on my right...

Justin Olaf.

Julie-Ann Olaf on my right ... and he definitely speaks English, you're sure
   of that?

Justin Apparently.

Julie-Ann Well, I do hope so.

Justin Mind you, it doesn't really matter to my mother. None of the men she
   lives with ever gets a word in, anyway.

Julie-Ann So it's this Olaf on my right—I hope your mother doesn't talk too
   much——

Justin So do I.

Julie-Ann —you know, monopolise the conversation too much—then
   Mummy at the other end—with her back to the door, then you on her right
   and then next to you, your mother who will be on Daddy's left, of course.
   Have you got that?

Justin Daddy's left. Yes. I think so. (*He picks up the chairs again, but then
   hesitates*) Er ... Julie.

Julie-Ann (*absorbed with polishing the cutlery with a cloth*) Mmm?

Justin You're not ... we're not ... we're not in danger of going over the top
   a bit with all this, are we? You know, of making too big a thing of it?

Julie-Ann It is a big thing.

Justin Yes, well. Big-ish.

Julie-Ann The first time I'm going to meet your mother and her—current
   man. The first time you'll meet my parents. And the first time they'll all
   be meeting, too. It is important, Justy. It really is. It's very important.

Justin I just don't want it all—you know—to get out of proportion.

Julie-Ann No...

Justin Well. (*He makes to go again*)

Julie-Ann It's important for another reason as well, isn't it?

Justin What's that?

Julie-Ann We're going to—aren't we? We're going to—you know.
   Announce it. Our—you know—(*softly*)—engagement.

Justin Oh, yes. Right.

Julie-Ann Have you thought what you're going to say yet?

Justin Say?

Julie-Ann You said you were going to make a speech.

Justin When?

Julie-Ann During dinner.

Justin I never said that.

Julie-Ann Yes, you did.

Justin When?

Julie-Ann The other night. In bed.

Justin Oh. Then. I thought that was a joke.

Julie-Ann I didn't take it as a joke. I thought it was a lovely idea.

Justin Ah.

Julie-Ann So romantic. It made me cry.

Justin Oh.

Julie-Ann I mean happy-cry. You know.

Justin Good.

Julie-Ann Not cry-cry. You are going to make a speech, aren't you, Justy?

Justin I'll—yes, I'll—say a few words, yes. Possibly.

Julie-Ann How we're both so in love—how happy we are together—how we want to share the rest of our lives with each other. For ever and ever...?

Justin Yes. Sure. Something along those lines...

Julie-Ann (*frowning at a fork*) This is disgusting. I can't believe we've been eating off these all this time, Justy. (*She scrubs with renewed vigour*)

Justin (*staring at her, a little worried*) Julie, listen, darling. No-one's going to notice. I promise.

Julie-Ann My mother certainly will.

Justin Ah. Yes.

Justin goes off with the chairs, briefly

Julie-Ann (*despairingly*) Filthy! They're all filthy! We could both have got typhoid, you know. That's the trouble with eating by candlelight all the time. You never notice the state of the cutlery.

A fresh gust of wind and rain at the window

(*Calling*) Is the bedroom window shut?

Justin (*off, inaudibly*) Hot?

Julie-Ann (*calling*) Is the bedroom window shut?

Justin returns empty-handed

Justin Sorry, what did you say?

Julie-Ann Is the window shut? In the bedroom?

Justin Yes, I said I closed it.

Julie-Ann We don't want another flood, do we?

Justin returns to the window

Justin I think it's getting worse out here.

Julie-Ann I hope your mother gets here all right.

Justin She'll be all right. Olaf's driving her. They're only coming from Godalming.

Julie-Ann I hope we haven't forgotten anything, that's all. I just pray I haven't forgotten anything.

Justin Julie, darling, stop worrying. Calm down. It's all going to be a great evening, I promise you. They'll all get on fine. I'll love your parents, you'll adore my mother. They'll all fall in love with each other. It's only a party, Julie. That's all. Now relax, darling. All right?

Julie-Ann (*unconvincingly*) I just want them to love you, Justy. As much as I do. (*She smiles and kisses him*) Well. Nearly as much, anyway. (*She pauses slightly*) You'll—er... You'll try to remember not to call me Julie while they're here, won't you, Justy?

Justin What?

Julie-Ann I told you they hate me being called Julie. I did tell you.

Justin I didn't think you were serious. What am I supposed to call you, then?

Julie-Ann Julie-Ann. That's what they prefer.

Justin Is that what you prefer?

Julie-Ann I don't mind...

Justin Why should I call you Julie-Ann?

Julie-Ann Please.

Justin I've never called you Julie-Ann.

Julie-Ann Just for tonight. For their sake. Please.

Justin Well, I'll try and remember.

Julie-Ann Don't sulk, Justy. Don't sulk, darling.

Justin Look... We're putting ourselves out quite a bit one way or another, aren't we? For your parents? I mean, first of all we have to move everything of yours out of the flat, I've reorganised my study...

Julie-Ann We had to move my things out—if my parents knew we'd been living together they'd just die—with shock.

Justin Why? God, you're twenty-whatever-it-is. You're not a kid, Julie. You're a grown woman.

Julie-Ann That doesn't come into it as far as they're concerned. They don't see it that way, not at all.

Justin Why on earth not?

Julie-Ann (*awkwardly*) Because I'm still—Being the youngest. They still look on me as—their—as the baby, if you like. You know what I mean.

Justin (*faintly incredulous*) Their baby?

Julie-Ann In a way.

Justin Then it's time they grew up too, isn't it?

Julie-Ann Listen, Justy, you have to understand. My eldest sister, Lucy-Jane, she had this terrible row with them and then moved to Canada. She never communicates from one year to the next and they refuse to have her name mentioned in the house. My other sister, Sally-Jo—she married this man they both—disapprove of—and now she's moved to Truro—so they never see each other either. I'm all they have left, Justy. They need me.

Justin They have each other, don't they?

Julie-Ann But they need me.

Justin So do I, Julie.

Julie-Ann (*softly*) I know you do. And I need you, Justy. I really, really do. You know that.

They hold each other, happy for a second

You'll love them. I know you will. You'll get on so well.

Justin They do sound just the slightest bit heavy-going.

Julie-Ann No. Never. My father's the funniest person I know. He makes me laugh more than anyone in the world. Apart from you, of course.

Justin What about your mother?

Julie-Ann Oh, you'll love her, Justy. She's exactly like me. Everyone says so. (*She glances at the clock*) Oh, we must get on. Look at the time. (*She takes up the tray of cutlery and starts to head off to the dining room*) Do you think your mother will mind me calling you Justy?

Justin No idea. I don't give a stuff if she does, quite frankly.

Julie-Ann I can call you Justin, if you'd rather. Just for tonight.

Justin Don't bother. We can't both be sitting there all evening trying to remember each other's name.

Julie-Ann (*going*) All right. I just wondered. Don't get sulky, now.

Julie-Ann goes off, singing, as before

Justin stands frowning. The phone rings

Justin (*answering*) Hallo... Oh hallo, Mother... Are you just setting out?... What?... Listen, you can have one when you get here, Mother, why don't you wait till you get here?... Well, Olaf can wait, can't he? Especially if he's driving. I don't care if he's a rally driver, he still shouldn't drink, should he?... Mother, just get in the car, please. ... Yes, I love you, too. See you soon. 'Bye.

Julie-Ann enters during the following. The tray is now empty

(*Ringing off, a small prayer*) Please, please, God. Behave yourself tonight.

Julie-Ann Who was that?
Justin My mother. She's just setting off.
Julie-Ann Oh. Cutting it fine, isn't she?

Slight pause

Justy—I'm going to say something. And I don't want you to get cross with me.
Justin Cross?
Julie-Ann Promise me you won't get grumpy.
Justin Why?
Julie-Ann It's just that—now that I've moved all my things out of here and back to my own flat—all my belongings... I've been thinking seriously about this. I think things should stay that way, for now.
Justin How do you mean?
Julie-Ann I don't think we should live together any more. Not until we're married.
Justin What?
Julie-Ann All I'm saying is——
Justin Julie, we've been living together for six months.
Julie-Ann I know. That's the point. And I don't think we should any longer, you see. Not now we've decided to get married.
Justin I don't follow this at all.
Julie-Ann Well, otherwise, I was thinking about this, otherwise there won't be anything special about getting married, will there? It'll just be the same as before. I want being married to be something special, Justy.
Justin It will be special. Of course it will.
Julie-Ann How will it be?
Justin Well, we'll have made vows to each other. I don't know, we'll have rings—and—go on honeymoon... (*He trails off*) Tax—and so on...
Julie-Ann How different is that? We can go on holiday now—we can wear rings if we wanted to—we can make promises... I want it to be different...
Justin I don't know what this is about. Are you saying we're not even going to sleep together?
Julie-Ann That's the point. Not till we're married.
Justin We're not getting married till the twenty-third of June.
Julie-Ann That's not long.
Justin It's three months away, Julie!
Julie-Ann That'll fly by.
Justin This is crazy.
Julie-Ann Darling, think what it'll be like.
Justin I am. It'll be terrible.
Julie-Ann I mean, on the honeymoon night. When we haven't touched each other—like that—for all that time. It'll be fantastic, won't it?

Justin I'll probably have forgotten how to do it.

Julie-Ann Justy! You won't. And if you have, my darling, I'll soon remind you. I have this fantasy, you see. Let me tell you. We'll get on the plane together at Heathrow. And we'll fly to Barbados. But when we get to the airport, we'll both take separate taxis to the hotel, you see.

Justin Separate—?

Julie-Ann Shhh, wait! And I'll arrive first and I'll check in and go straight to the room where I'll have a bath and I'll change into my evening dress and I'll make myself really beautiful for you and then I'll take my book down to the lounge and I'll——

Justin Your book? You're reading a book on our honeymoon night?

Julie-Ann Wait! I haven't finished! And I'll sit in the lounge and wait. And pretend to read. Only the words will probably be a blur because I'll just be so excited with anticipation. And, in the meantime, you'll go up to the room and have your bath and get changed and make yourself handsome and desirable for me. And when you're ready, you'll come down to the lounge and in a moment you'll notice me all alone in the corner, a solitary beautiful woman absorbed in her book. I'll be unaware of you initially and then— quite suddenly—I'll become conscious of your stare—and for a fleeting second, our eyes will meet and, a few moments later, you'll be there, this tall figure standing over me, looking down. And you'll introduce yourself and offer to buy me a drink. I may be a little hesitant about accepting at first, but eventually, I'll agree——

Justin Glad to hear it.

Julie-Ann And for the rest of that magical evening we'll be like two strangers, gradually getting acquainted, growing ever closer and closer, increasingly filled with an aching longing for each other. A candle-lit dinner under the stars, caviar, lobster, delicious wine and then finally, when we can scarcely contain ourselves, up to the bedroom. And we'll both undress and explore each other's body, first with our eyes, then our hands until finally we're making perfect love together as if for the first time in our lives yet having known each other for ever. Can't you imagine it, darling?

Silence

Justin What book are you currently reading? (*He pauses*) Yes, well, it sounds all right in theory but——

Julie-Ann It'll be so beautiful.

Justin What are we supposed to do in the meantime? I mean, between now and June.

Julie-Ann We'll dream of each other, darling. I'll dream of you. You'll dream of me.

Justin I'll probably be doing a bloody sight more than that.

Julie-Ann Justy!

Justin Julie, we've been doing it—we've been having sex together—well, several times a week, haven't we…? On average.

Julie-Ann I've no idea. I don't go counting, do I…?

Justin Well, nor do I. But the point is, Julie, you can't suddenly stop just like that and become a monk overnight. It's like smoking—you have to give up gradually. Otherwise you get—you know—withdrawal symptoms.

Julie-Ann (*sadly*) So you won't agree to it?

Justin I don't—it would—it would be very—difficult. That's all I'm saying.

Julie-Ann It would be just as difficult for me.

Justin I'm sure.

Julie-Ann The only difference is, that I'm prepared to do it for you. But you aren't apparently for me. (*She moves away*)

Justin Oh, come on, that's not fair. That's like me saying, OK, Julie, are you prepared to be hung upside down from Tower Bridge for three days just to prove you love me? Because I'm very happy to do it for you, darling!

Julie-Ann Now you're just being silly.

Justin Not at all.

Julie-Ann (*rather coolly*) And it's Julie-Ann, please. Not Julie. I'm going to lay the table, excuse me.

Julie-Ann goes

Justin Oh, come on! (*He stands miserably*) Come on, three months. Men aren't designed for that. No way.

Julie-Ann returns clutching five dessert forks. She appears a trifle distraught. The beginnings of a panic attack

What's wrong?

Julie-Ann I thought you said you had six of everything?

Justin I thought I did.

Julie-Ann There's only five pudding forks. (*She goes to the cutlery drawer and rummages around in it*)

Justin, alarmed, goes to help her

Justin Are you sure? I thought I had six of everything… My mother gave me six of everything originally, I'm sure she did.

Not finding whatever it is she's looking for, Julie-Ann tries one or two other drawers

Julie-Ann (*a trace hysterical*) Well, you haven't got six pudding forks. There's only five. Look for yourself.

Justin Well, I did have. (*He opens drawers at random*) Now don't—make a crisis of it... We'll find it. We'll find it, don't worry... Probably just slipped down the back of the—somewhere...
Julie-Ann You won't find it, it's not here.

Justin begins to search the kitchen for the missing fork, looking in progressively more unlikely places. Julie-Ann gives up and stands for a second

Now what are we going to do? The whole table's going to look ridiculous, isn't it?
Justin Of course it isn't.
Julie-Ann What are we going to do? What are we going to do?
Justin Julie! Don't get like this, darling. It doesn't help! We'll find it. Forks don't walk, do they?
Julie-Ann I'm just going to have to go out and buy one, aren't I?
Justin It's half past six—what are you talking about?
Julie-Ann I'm not sitting down to dinner with a fork missing...
Justin (*sitting her down*) Julie, sit down and pull yourself together. You know why you're like this. You know. You get these moods, you know you do, darling. You're getting hysterical for no reason.
Julie-Ann I'm going to have to go out, I'm going to have to go out now, aren't I? Go searching for forks.
Justin Julie, it's pouring with rain, everywhere round here is closed, where the hell are you going to buy a fork at this time of night?
Julie-Ann (*getting up*) Then I'll have to borrow one. I'll ask round the other flats. Someone's bound to have a spare.
Justin (*angrily*) My God, Julie, every month it's the same! Listen to yourself! No-one's even going to notice.
Julie-Ann Of course they will.
Justin Who the hell is going to notice there's a fork missing?
Julie-Ann My mother for one!
Justin Well, bugger your mother!

Julie-Ann freezes. Silence

(*Shocked at his own outburst*) I'm sorry, Julie. I'm really sorry. I didn't mean to say that. I'm deeply, deeply sorry. Really. Please, believe me.

Julie-Ann, grim-faced, goes to the front door

I really—can't even begin to say how sorry I am for saying that. I mean, your mother, for God's sake. Your *mother*. It's appalling of me. I'm so, so, so sorry, Julie. Ann. Truly.

Julie-Ann (*coolly*) I hope you will not be using language like that in front of my parents.

Justin I said I——

Julie-Ann Perhaps you'd care to turn the oven on to low whilst I'm out. I'll leave the door on the latch. Try not to lock me out, please.

Julie-Ann sweeps out and closes the door

Justin stands unhappily. He looks out of the windows. The wind and rain continue unabated

Justin (*half to himself*) Mr and Mrs Jobson... Derek and Dee—Mother—Julie-Ann and I have some really wonderful news ... we are planning to get married in June ... and in order to celebrate this happy event—we're giving up sex for twelve bloody weeks. Oh, God...

The phone rings

(*Answering*) Hallo ... oh, hallo, Mother ... what? ... Why have you stopped at the pub? ... Look, it's nearly. ... Well, tell Olaf to get back in the car... You're supposed to be here in... Mother, please. Do not have another drink... No, you don't... You don't need one at all ... just get in the car and please be here. (*He rings off*) God! (*He remembers*) Oven. (*He goes into the kitchen and stands at the stove. Staring at the stove, gloomily*) Twelve weeks? I might as well stick my head in this oven and have done with it. What's there to live for? What's there to live for...?

Faintly, from outside the doors above the noise of the storm, a woman's long-drawn-out scream as if falling from some height. Justin turns, startled, and goes into the sitting-room, forgetting the oven

Outside the windows we see that someone is gripping the balcony rail, hanging on for grim death as they hang above the river

Justin stares in amazement

Slowly and painfully, with great difficulty, the someone now hauls themself up a little so that their head is visible over the rail. It is Paige, a woman in her late twenties. She is soaked to the skin from the torrential rain. Her hair is plastered to her head like an otter. She has blood on her face, hands and legs. Her make-up is streaked and her clothes are badly torn

Justin stares at her, horrified

Outside the window, Paige's mouth opens and closes, but her words are drowned out by the storm which rages outside. She is shouting something silently. Although we can't hear her it looks suspiciously like "Help!"

(*Reacting at last, calling*) Just a minute. (*He fumbles with the window locks—and eventually opens one window*)

The full force of the storm is heard. Justin is practically blown backwards. He fights his way on to the balcony, forcing himself forward against the wind. He reaches Paige and, with difficulty, hauls her over the rail. She is completely exhausted and he has to catch her before she drops in a heap on the balcony. He half-assists, half-carries her into the flat

My God! Here. You lie here——(*He considers putting her on the sofa but decides, given her damp and bloody condition and the light nature of his sofa fabric, not to do that*) No, hang on. Lie down here a second. (*He lays her out on the floor*)

Paige, semi-conscious, groans in pain as he does so

I'll—fetch a towel—a blanket. I'll fetch something. Wait there! Don't try to move.

Justin darts off, momentarily, to the bedroom

Paige tries to sit up. It is evidently agony to do so. She lies back down again

Justin returns. He has a large bath towel and a blanket

Just a second. (*He spreads the blanket on the sofa, leaves the towel on the coffee table and returns his attention to Paige*) Listen. I'm going to lift you on to the sofa, OK? (*He prises her gently off the floor*)

Paige yelps with pain

(*Moving her*) I probably shouldn't be doing this, moving you at all, but what the hell, I must've done all the damage I can do already. (*He sits Paige on the sofa*) How's that?
Paige (*in pain*) Hah!
Justin How did you get there?
Paige (*in pain*) Hah!
Justin Did you climb up out of the river?
Paige (*in pain*) Hah!

Justin You're half-drowned.
Paige (*in pain*) Hah!
Justin God, you're not a failed suicide, are you?
Paige (*trying to laugh, but still in pain*) Hah, hah, hah!
Justin Are you in much pain?
Paige (*reacting to the idiocy of such a question*) Haaahh!
Justin Listen, I have a rudimentary knowledge of first aid. Can you try and describe where it hurts? Where does it hurt most?
Paige (*with difficulty*) Every ... where...
Justin Ah. (*He proffers the towel*) Would you like to—I'm frightened you'll get cold...
Paige I'm—sodding—freezing...
Justin Yes, right. Perhaps I could pull the—(*reacting to her state of semi-nudity*)—perhaps you should pull the blanket round you a little.

Paige does so, half-heartedly

(*Handing her the towel*) Here. I think I'd better call an ambulance, hadn't I?
Paige (*despite her condition, quite vehemently*) No!
Justin (*startled*) What?
Paige No ambulances! No ambulances!
Justin Why not? You need medical atten——
Paige (*trying to stand, but failing*) I have to go. I have to get out of here.
Justin Please, sit down. You're in no condition to move. Really.
Paige He'll find me. If he finds me here...
Justin Who?
Paige Micky.
Justin Micky?
Paige Micky upstairs.
Justin Micky upstairs? Who's Micky upstairs?
Paige Well, he was upstairs. He's probably halfway downstairs by now.
Justin Downstairs? Why's he halfway downstairs?
Paige Looking for me.
Justin (*confused*) I see. And why is he coming downstairs looking for you?
Paige Because I should be upstairs.
Justin Why should you be upstairs?
Paige Because that's where I live.
Justin Then what are you doing downstairs? How did you get downstairs?
Paige I climbed out of the window, didn't I?
Justin Good God!
Paige From the penthouse. I managed to climb down two floors. And then I fell.
Justin Fell?

Paige Yes.

Justin You fell four floors?

Paige I'd have been in the bloody river if I hadn't managed to grab your rail.

Justin But what made you climb out in the first place, for God's sake?

Paige Because I wasn't sitting there waiting for him to come back, was I?

Justin Him? You mean Micky?

Paige No, not Micky. Rudy.

Justin Rudy? Who's Rudy? Is Rudy upstairs as well?

Paige No, Rudy's in Birmingham, the bastard.

Justin Birmingham? Who is he, then?

Paige Rudy's my bastard boyfriend. So-called.

Justin Then who's Micky?

Paige (*wearily*) Micky works for Rudy. Rudy locked me in my room. Rudy's gone to Birmingham with Winston. He left Micky to keep an eye on me. All right? Happy?

Justin Why should he lock you in your room?

Paige Because he wants me there when he comes back.

Justin I see. And might you not have been?

Paige No way, brother. He's planning to beat the shit out of me.

Justin Hit you?

Paige Putting it mildly.

Justin My God, he can't do that.

Paige Really? You want to tell him that? Rudy is nine feet high. Which is only a foot shorter than his mate Winston. You fancy going to tell him?

Justin I'll—we could certainly report him. He can't do that!

Paige He's Rudy Raven, darling.

Justin Rudy—?

Paige Don't tell me you never heard of Rudy Raven?

Justin Can't say I have.

Paige Then you are very, very lucky and keep it that way. I wish I hadn't. I mean, don't get me wrong, I'm not soft, I can put up with an occasional slapping, I can cope with that. I've had plenty of that. I had this shining example from my dad, bless him. But wire coat hangers—I draw the line there. That's something else again.

Justin (*shocked*) Wire coat hangers? I don't believe it.

Paige Want to look?

Justin No, no.

Paige If he comes back and I'm still there, he'll kill me. I know he will. Bloody near killed me before he left as it was.

Justin Why?

Paige You know, I clean forgot to ask him. Listen, would you help me, please? You look a decent bloke. I don't need much. Just a little help. Please.

Justin I don't see how I can——
Paige Please. I'm begging you. Please.
Justin But surely, isn't this a matter for the police? He can't go around ...
it doesn't matter who he ... I mean, I'm happy to——
Paige The police? Listen, Rudy is drinking mates with most of them. He gets
them ringside seats. They're not going to go after him, are they? Most of
them are on his side. If they're not in his pocket.
Justin Ringside seats?
Paige Rudy Raven, darling, come on. The boxing promoter. As in Raven
Enterprises. (*Muttering*) As in raven madman. Everyone's heard of him.
Justin I don't follow boxing.
Paige Really? You're the first man I've met who doesn't. First straight man,
anyway. I take it you're straight?
Justin Yes.
Paige If you don't follow boxing, what do you do?
Justin Do? I'm a—software designer.
Paige Software?
Justin Computer games.
Paige (*mildly impressed*) Oh. I see. Well.
Justin I'm quite fond of cricket.
Paige Cricket? Oh dear, you sad man. Listen, are you going to help me or
not? Because Micky'll be banging on that door in a minute.
Justin Well, we won't let him in.
Paige Listen, if Micky Rale bangs on that door, love, he'll be in and so will
the bloody door, all right?
Justin Ah. He's—big as well, is he? I... Well, I... What exactly do you
want?
Paige Thank you. I need some dry clothes. If you've got a pair of jeans or
an old T-shirt I can borrow, I'm not fussy. Just something to keep me dry.
And I also need a little bit of money. Not a lot. Just to get me to Hounslow.
I've got a girl friend in Hounslow. She'll take me in, I know she will, just
overnight till I can get out of London. I'll pay you back. I swear I will. And
I'll even post you back your clothes. Word of honour.

Slight pause

Justin All right.
Paige Ta.
Justin We'd—better be quick, then... My—girlfriend, she'll be back in a
minute, she——
Paige You got a girlfriend, then?
Justin Yes. She's a programmer. Computers as well.
Paige Yes? You must have fun evenings together. Coming round, is she?

Justin Yes, she's just—she's just popped out to look for a fork.

Paige A what?

Justin A fork. A dessert fork.

Paige A fork! I thought you said something else for a minute. (*She smiles*)

Justin (*laughing a little nervously*) No.

Paige I mean, if you're here, she doesn't need to go out for a takeaway, surely?

Justin (*laughing some more*) I hope not.

Paige I'm Paige, by the way. P-A-I-G-E. Paige Petite. That's my professional name, anyway.

Justin Hallo. Justin. Justin Lazenby.

Paige How do you do, Justin?

Justin (*increasingly intrigued by her*) How do you do?

Paige tries to get up. She is still weak

(*Springing to help her*) Here.

Paige God, I'm going to be blue all over in the morning.

Justin From the fall?

Paige Some of it. My arse is like a bloody zebra crossing. All right, I can manage now.

Justin You're still shivering. Perhaps you should have a quick bath first. Just to warm you up.

Paige No, there isn't time, I'll——

Justin No, you're still absolutely frozen. You shouldn't go out again till you've warmed up, honestly. There's time for a bath. I'll run you one. Please.

Paige (*studying him*) I reckon your girlfriend's a very lucky girl.

Justin (*modestly*) Well... Ready? This way.

Paige seems to have gathered her strength. Justin guides her towards the bedroom

Paige She coming for supper then, is she?

Justin Yes.

Paige That's why she's looking for a fork, right?

Justin Well, we have several other people coming, actually. My mother, her mother and father, a friend of my mother's——

Paige My God! I'd better be quick, then. I'll be mothered out.

Justin It's OK. They're not due for a little while...

Paige and Justin go off

A brief pause. We hear the bath running

Julie-Ann enters through the front door, wild-eyed, breathless and forkless

She searches round and retrieves her handbag from under the coffee table. She rummages for her car keys

Justin enters from the bedroom

(Rather surprised to find her here) Ah!

Julie-Ann *(taking her coat from the peg)* I'm driving up to the supermarket. Would you believe there's nobody at home in this whole building. Or nobody who's prepared to answer. I even tried the penthouse.

Justin Julie, there's been a bit of——

Julie-Ann I'll be five minutes. Then I'll have to get changed. Could you take my dress out of its hanging bag? I meant to do that earlier. It'll be creased to death otherwise...

Justin Yes, Julie, I just have to tell you——

Julie-Ann Are you running a bath?

Justin Yes, that's what I wanted to——

Julie-Ann Can you run one for me afterwards? I've been rushing up and down those stairs, I'm unbelievably hot...

Justin Listen, why don't you just——

Julie-Ann Have you turned the oven on? *(She moves to the stove)* You haven't even turned the oven on. Honestly, I ask you to do one little thing, Justy—— *(She frenziedly adjusts the oven dial)*

Justin I was going to turn it on, darling. I really was. Only this extraordinary thing happened. This——

Julie-Ann I'll be back. You can tell me then. See you in a minute. God, look at the time, look at the time. Do the glasses! Put out the glasses.

Julie-Ann, now with her coat on, bag and keys in hand, hurries out, closing the door behind her. In her hurry, she again leaves it on the latch

Justin sighs. The phone rings

Justin *(answering)* Hallo ... where are you now? ... Yes, I'm sure it is ... yes... I'm so pleased... Listen, Mother, are you sure he's a rally driver? ... Well, I don't think rally drivers usually get completely rat-arsed, do they? ... Well, Mother, please make this one your last. Please, you promised me, Mother... Yes, I know I am... Well, sorry about that... Some of us are born boring. See you later. *(He rings off)* Oh, God. I have a bad feeling about this.

Justin picks up the tray, goes to the bar and starts to select six wine glasses and six water glasses and carries these off to the dining room

Pause. The doorbell rings. A beat

Justin returns, listens for a second, thinks he must have misheard and goes off

The doorbell rings again. A beat. The door is opened

Micky enters. He is in his forties, well built. He wears a smart suit. He is an ex-boxer but, from the visible evidence, one who was on the losing end of most of his bouts

He inspects the flat. He moves to the windows and, opening them, steps briefly out into the night. The wind and rain still continue. Micky peers over the balcony, searching for signs of Paige

At this moment, Paige, straight from her quick bath, returns from the bedroom. She is wearing what is evidently Julie-Ann's intended dinner dress. It is a proper, little-girl, demure sort of dress

Paige *(as she enters)* Justin, I hope you don't mind, I found this dress in the wardrobe and I—— *(She realizes no-one is in the room)* Oh. *(She turns and calls)* Justin! *(She sees the open windows)* What are you doing out here? It's bloody freezing. You'll catch your death—oh, my God!

Micky steps back through the windows. He grabs her wrist in one hand and closes the windows behind him

Micky Come on——
Paige Micky! Let go!
Micky Come on, back you come!
Paige Micky, will you let go of me, please. You are breaking my bloody wrist.
Micky You coming, then?
Paige Let go!
Micky Are you coming?
Paige Not till you let go!

Micky considers and finally releases Paige's wrist

(Rubbing her arm) God! I've got another set of bruises now. You stupid gorilla!
Micky Upstairs, all right?
Paige No.

Micky (*tense again*) What?

Paige I'm not staying up there, Micky. You saw what mood he was in. I stay there till Rudy comes back, he'll bloody kill me. He's mad, Micky, you've seen what he's like. He's completely lost it, hasn't he? Do you want him to kill me? Is that what you want to happen?

Micky If you're not up there when he comes back, he'll kill me.

Paige Listen, I escaped. It wasn't your fault. You'd checked on me regular. You'd kept my door locked. What more could you have done? Nothing. You didn't know this silly bitch was going to climb out of a sixth-floor window, did you? It wasn't your fault.

Micky Rudy won't see it that way.

Paige Look, you were innocently watching a porn video. How were you expected to know?

Micky It wasn't a porn video.

Paige Well, whatever.

Micky *Rambo*. I was watching *Rambo*.

Paige What, again? How many times have you seen that, then?

Micky Fifty-six times. Ten in the cinema. Now, you coming?

Paige Micky. Please. I'm pleading with you. Please.

Micky Come on, Paige. You don't want me to force you.

Paige I didn't do anything, Micky. I swear I didn't.

Micky I don't know anything about it.

Paige Do you think I'm that stupid? Start sleeping around behind Rudy's back? I know what he's like, Micky. Do you really think I'm mad enough to do something like that? Risk pissing him off?

Micky That's between you and Rudy. Nothing to do with me.

Paige So you're just going to stand by, are you? Let him do what he wants? Be accessory to murder? I thought we were friends, Micky.

Micky We're friends, yes. But I'm—my loyalty's to Rudy. I mean, I couldn't deceive him, Paige. I owe him. We both owe him.

Paige Not me. No way. Anything I owe to Rudy I have repaid with interest, Micky. As far as I'm concerned, my account is now in credit…

Micky Come on, Paige, don't make me force you——

Paige All right, Micky, here's how it goes. You are probably three times heavier than me and no doubt ten times as strong. But if you touch me I will put up such a fight—it will make your brief and disastrous boxing career seem like a bloody Brownies' pillow fight——

Micky Disastrous? It wasn't disastrous…

Paige I heard, Micky, I heard. Rudy told me. What was it? Twenty-three fights, one win, three draws and nineteen losses…

Micky Bollocks…

Paige Oh, and one knockout. And that was the referee.

Micky That was an accident. He was getting on my tits.

Paige Got you disqualified for life though, didn't it?

Micky I don't want to discuss it. That's a closed chapter. Come on, Paige.

Paige I mean it, Micky. I won't come without a fight.

Micky (*shrugging*) All right—if that's how you want it... (*He starts to move towards her*)

Paige You're going to have to hurt me, Micky. And when I tell Rudy, he's not going to like that, is he?

Micky (*stopping*) What?

Paige You know how he feels about other people touching me.

Micky This is different.

Paige Listen. He's accused me of carrying on with someone. And he's told me to come up with a name by the time he gets back. Or else. What if I was to name you, Micky? What do you think he'd do to you?

Micky You wouldn't do that. (*He stares at her*) Would you?

Paige What have I got to lose? I don't want to die. I'll have to come up with a name eventually, won't I? You, Winston, the Pope. Anyone. It might as well be you.

Micky You can't.

Paige Try me.

Micky He'd never believe you.

Paige Ah, but would he believe *you*, Micky? That's the point.

Silence

I'm not going up there. That's final...

Micky Well, I'm not going up without you.

Paige Deadlock then.

Micky (*with a sudden idea*) I'll phone Rudy.

Paige I wouldn't. It's nearly fight time. He doesn't like people calling him around fight time, does he?

Micky I'll call him later on, then.

Paige You do that. I won't be here.

Micky You're not leaving. You can stay down here if you want. But you're not leaving this building. I can't let you do that, Paige.

Paige We can't stay here, can we?

Micky Why not?

Paige Because it's someone else's flat, you fool.

Micky Whose flat is it, anyway?

Justin comes in. He has now changed into his smart party gear. He stops as he sees them

Justin Oh.

Paige Hallo, Justin. This is Micky.
Justin Hallo.
Paige Micky, this is Justin.

Micky stares at Justin

Justin (*to Paige*) Er—are you...?
Paige Fine.
Justin I mean, do you want me to call...?
Paige No. No way.

Pause. Justin looks at Micky. Micky looks at Justin. Paige looks at them both

Justin Well...
Paige Justin... Would it be all right if—me and Micky stayed for a little bit?
Justin Stayed?
Paige Down here. Just for a little while. Would you mind?
Justin Here?
Paige Only it's a little inconvenient for us both to leave just at present.
Justin (*rather nervously*) I see. Well, I'm afraid it's not all that convenient for us if you stay. I mean, Julie and I have this dinner party, you see. We're expecting her parents and my mother and a friend of my mother's. Quite soon, actually. So. I mean, much as I'd like to... Sorry.

Pause

Paige Actually, Justin. I don't think there's a choice.
Justin Now look, I... (*He stares at them*)
Paige Sorry, Justin. It's—what do you call it? Accomplished.
Justin It is? Listen, I...

The front door opens. Julie-Ann enters, triumphantly brandishing a fork. She starts taking off her coat

Julie-Ann Got one! Would you believe, they had one! It's not a perfect match but it'll do—— (*She sees Paige and Micky*) Oh. Who are you?
Justin This is Paige and Micky from upstairs. They've—just dropped in.
Julie-Ann (*with barely a glance at them*) Oh. Hallo.
Paige Hallo.
Justin This is my fiancée, Julie. Ann.
Julie-Ann (*barely stopping*) Yes, well, I'm afraid I'm running very late. I need to have a bath and get changed for dinner. Do excuse me. We're expecting guests very shortly. I'd love to stay and chat. Excuse me.

Julie-Ann goes. A pause. A fork is dropped. She comes back

(*Staring at Paige*) Is that my dress?

Pause

That's my dress.

Pause

She's wearing my dress. You're wearing my dress.
Paige Sorry about that...
Julie-Ann Would you take that dress off immediately, please. Why is she wearing my dress? Justin, tell her to take my dress off at once.
Justin Er...
Julie-Ann How dare you wear my dress! How dare you!
Paige I'm very sorry about this. You're welcome to borrow one of mine.
Julie-Ann One of yours?
Paige If you'd like.
Julie-Ann I don't want one of yours. I want my own.
Paige If you go upstairs to the penthouse. In my bedroom you'll find a whole wardrobe of them. I've got dozens.
Julie-Ann Then why aren't you wearing one of them?
Paige There are technical reasons.
Julie-Ann I'm not wearing one of yours.
Justin Julie...
Julie-Ann (*angrily*) No! Why should I want to wear one of yours? Give me one good reason! One good reason!
Micky Listen. Here's a good reason. (*He produces a rather impressive-looking gun from inside his jacket and puts it on the bar*)

The others stare at it. Julie-Ann squeaks nervously

Julie-Ann Ah!
Justin (*softly*) Oh, my God.
Paige Micky, do you have to?
Micky (*to Julie-Ann*) Now you go upstairs like a good girl and you find yourself a nice dress like this lady's kindly offered and you get changed and then you come straight back down here again, right? You do just that. No more, no less, right? Because if you don't, then I will pick up this great big gun and (*he points at Justin*) I will blow his fucking head off! (*Fiercely*) NOW, GET UPSTAIRS!
Julie-Ann (*in sheer terror*) Justin...

Justin Do as the man says, Julie.

Julie-Ann hurries to the door, whimpering slightly

Micky Oy!
Julie-Ann (*jumping*) What?
Micky Keys! (*He tosses her a key ring*) Now, shift your arse!

Julie-Ann scuttles out

Micky picks up the gun and puts it back in the holster

Now then. I understand you're having a supper party?
Justin (*very nervously*) Yes, that's right.
Micky Right. Anything we can do to help, then?

As Justin stares at them both, the Lights fade to Black-out

SCENE 2

The same. A few minutes later

There is now a saucepan of soup heating on the stove which Justin, having temporarily shed his jacket and donned an apron, is stirring

Paige appears, followed closely by Micky. They remain very much inseparable throughout all this; wherever she decides to go, he follows

Paige That smells good.
Justin Spicy mushroom soup. My own version.
Micky I can't eat mushrooms.
Paige Bad luck. (*To Justin*) So you're a chef, then? As well as a computer man?
Justin Not really what you'd term a chef. Just soups.
Paige Ah, I see. You make a lot of soups, then, do you?
Justin No, not really. Just spicy mushroom.
Micky I can't eat spice.
Paige What a shame.
Micky I've got a damaged stomach lining.
Paige Along with everything else. Listen, we brought the extra chairs from the bedroom...
Justin Thank you.

Paige And listen, I worked it out with the cutlery. Now there's the eight of us, if some of them use their soup spoons again for the pudding and some of them does without a pudding fork altogether and just uses it for the main course and they wipes their knife from the main course once they've used it then they can use it again for the cheese and if they want to spread their rolls as well then they can always use them little butter knives, can't they? And the rest of it we can eat with our fingers.

Justin Oh, my God!

Paige That sound all right?

Justin Brilliant.

Paige What else we having, then?

Justin Well, we've ordered in the main course, I'm afraid. Bit of a cop-out but otherwise you spend the whole evening in the kitchen, don't you?

Paige I don't know. I never have. We always order out. If we're ever in. Our stove's still got the cardboard round it.

Justin As a matter of fact, they should be delivering in a minute. I've got the oven on ready. It's a chicken dish. Hope you like chicken.

Micky I only eat steak.

Paige Tragic.

Justin Julie's made the pudding. It's in the fridge there. Kiwi Mousse Surprise. That's her speciality.

Micky I can't eat foreign.

Paige Anything else we can do?

Justin Oh, yes… Salt and pepper. (*He indicates them*) Could you…? On the table.

Paige (*taking them*) Right.

Paige moves off. Micky follows

You going to follow me everywhere, are you?

Micky Yes.

Paige Terrific. Why don't you carry the salt, then? (*She hands it to him*)

Paige goes off, with Micky close behind her

Justin goes to the fridge and takes out two bottles of good white wine. He goes to the bar, hesitates, glances towards the bedrooms and makes an impulsive bid for freedom through the front door. It is locked with the mortice. Justin rattles the door handle vainly

Micky returns with Paige in tow

Justin looks sheepish. Micky holds up the front door mortice key. Justin goes and fetches the corkscrew from behind the bar

Looks lovely in there. Really nice.

Justin Good.

Paige Want us to light the candles?

Justin (*starting to open the bottles*) Not yet. Wait till they all arrive.

Paige Fair enough. (*She watches Justin for a moment*) Important dinner, then, is it?

Justin Fairly important, yes.

Paige Meeting the family?

Justin Right.

Paige You must love her a lot, do you? Going through all this. You must do.

Justin (*rather startled by her directness*) Er—yes. Yes, I do.

Paige Not natural for a bloke, is it? Otherwise. All this. How long you been together, then?

Justin Oh, about six months. We work together.

Paige I've been with Rudy five years.

Justin (*surprised*) That long?

Paige I was—dancing in this club and he asked me over afterwards.

Justin I see.

Paige We had champagne. Real stuff. Not the club's one.

Justin Right.

Paige Seventy-five quid a bottle.

Justin Hey!

Paige I got totally and utterly pissed. He had to drive me home.

Justin 'Dear..

Paige He didn't try anything, though. He could have done. I'd never even have noticed, I was that far gone, you know. Rudy just—saw me to my door and he said, I hope I can see you again sometime. You know, I really respected him for that. Most buggers would have been all over you, taking advantage, trying to get their money's worth. No, I really respected Rudy for that. Because I felt he really respected me. (*She pauses*) How bloody wrong can you get, eh?

A silence. She seems about to cry. Justin has stopped what he is doing and is watching her

(*Pulling herself together*) Sorry. I won't spoil your evening, I promise. (*To Micky*) Neither of us will, will we?

Micky (*suddenly, aggressively*) Where's that girlfriend of yours got to?

Paige She's choosing a dress, isn't she?

Micky Long time going about it.

Paige There's about seventy-five to choose from. (*To Justin*) So what's going to happen tonight, then? This is the first time you're all meeting up, is it?

Justin is now re-corking both bottles and putting them back in the fridge

Justin That's right. Actually, I'm... (*He hesitates*)
Paige What? You're what?
Justin It's tonight that I'll be—we're planning to formally announce our engagement. Name the day, you know. That's what we'd planned to do.
Paige Don't let us stop you, will you?
Justin (*looking at her*) No.

A moment. Then the doorbell rings

That might be Julie.
Paige Or your takeaway.
Justin I'd better go and see. (*Nervously, to Micky*) May I go and see?

Micky nods and hands Justin the key. Justin takes off his apron and goes to answer the front door. Micky and Paige wait in the living-room. Justin opens the door

It is Derek and Dee, Julie-Ann's parents, a Northern couple of quite exceptional conformity and seemingly permanent self-congratulatory manner

Derek Hallo, there.
Dee Hallo!
Derek You must be Justin?
Justin That's right.
Derek Derek. I'm Derek Jobson.
Justin Ah yes, hallo.
Derek This is my wife, Dee Jobson.
Dee Hallo, Justin. Dee Jobson. Pleased to meet you. I'm Derek's wife.
Justin Yes, please come in.
Dee Oh, isn't this nice? Lovely, isn't it, Derek?
Derek Very, very nice indeed, Dee. Ah.

The Jobsons stop as they see Paige and Micky

Justin Ah, yes. These are neighbours of mine. Can I introduce Paige and Micky who live upstairs.

Micky holds out his hand. Justin returns the key to him

This is—er—Derek and Dee.

Derek Derek Jobson, how do you do?
Paige Hallo.
Derek My wife Dee.
Dee Derek's wife.
Micky Hi.
Dee Oh yes, isn't this lovely?
Derek I see you've got weather down here as well, by the look of it.
Justin Yes.
Dee Look, you can see the river, Derek. Look. The River Thames.
Derek Well, I sincerely hope it is, Dee, for your sake. If it turns out to be the River Ouse, we can only blame your map-reading, eh? (*He laughs*)

Dee laughs. It is something the Jobsons do quite a lot of whenever Derek coins a new witticism. The others smile

Dee He's a laugh.
Justin Yes.
Dee There's some days I don't stop laughing from the minute I wake up. He knows what gets me going. He sometimes doesn't let up till bedtime. Do you, you devil? He's a laugh.
Justin Yes.

A pause. Justin laughs apropos of nothing very much. Another pause

(*At last*) How was your journey?
Derek Dreadful.
Dee Sixty-mile-an-hour crosswinds.
Derek Seventy. Had to lash her to the roof for ballast. (*He laughs*)

Dee laughs. Silence

Justin Would you both care for a drink? Er—Dee, can I get you something?
Dee Oh yes, I'll have—er... What'll I have? Yes, I'll have a—no—oh, I don't know. I'll have a—oh. I'll have—come back to me. Ask Derek.
Derek Small Scotch—tiny bit of water, no ice, please, Justin.
Justin Coming up.
Derek And if you have a single malt, Justin, I won't say no.
Justin Certainly have. Paige, I'm so sorry. Would you care for something?
Paige I'll have a large gin, thank you.
Justin Certainly. With tonic?
Paige Neat.
Justin (*doubtfully*) Right. Micky?
Micky I never drink.

Derek Sensible man.

Micky I get blinding headaches.

Justin (*starting to dispense the drinks*) Dee, have you decided yet?

Dee Yes, I have. I'll have a ... I'll have a ... oh ... I think I'll have a ... no...

Justin I'll come back to you. (*He hands Paige her drink*) Paige.

Paige Ta.

Derek Where's our Apple then? Where's our little Apple hiding?

Justin Sorry?

Dee Julie-Ann. We always call her our little Apple.

Derek Apple of our eye.

Justin Oh, I see.

Dee Little Apple. Still, as I said on the way down, didn't I, Derek? She can't stay on the tree for ever. She has to be plucked sooner or later.

Justin has a little problem pouring the drinks

Derek You're plucking our cream, Justin. You're plucking the cream of our crop, lad.

Justin Yes, well, sorry about that. Julie—Julie-Ann's just popped out for a— she'll be back in a second. (*He hands Derek his drink*) Er—Derek.

Derek Thank you very much.

Justin Now, Dee, have you decided yet?

Dee Er...

Derek The point is we've got the three daughters, Justin—I don't know if you know this—Lucy-Jane, the eldest, who we prefer never to mention, she's in Canada—enough said about that—and Sally-Jo who's now in the West Country and has formed what we consider an unsuitable relationship.

Dee Which we won't discuss.

Derek Which we won't discuss in polite company. So we're left with our youngest and brightest. Dream child, Justin. Wasn't she, Dee?

Dee A dream. Never cried. Never lost her temper.

Derek Never had a day's worry about her. Have we? Ever?

Dee Never. Unlike the other two...

Derek Well, the other two.

Dee Have you met our Julie-Ann—er—sorry, Paige, was it?

Paige Paige.

Dee Page. As in book?

Paige As in Three.

Dee Beg pardon. (*She puzzles over this*) No, you'll like Julie-Ann, Paige. She's a lovely girl. I don't think I know anyone who doesn't get on with her, do you, Derek?

Derek No-one I can think of.

Dee Unassuming, wonderful temperament, a little bit modest...

Derek A bit too modest sometimes.

Dee Well, possibly. Still, it's a fault in the right direction, isn't it?

Derek Oh, yes. I like modesty in a woman. (*He pauses*) Makes up for me. (*He laughs*)

Dee (*pealing with laughter*) Makes up for him.

They both laugh for a little

Oh dear. Do you both have children, Paige and—er—Micky?

Paige You must be joking.

Micky goes and re-locks the front door

Justin Paige is a dancer, so she...

Derek A dancer? Ah!

Paige Ex-dancer.

Derek Show business, eh? And what line are you in, Micky?

Micky Security.

Derek Oh, right. I approve of that.

Dee We need it, don't we?

Derek These days.

Dee It's everywhere.

Derek I blame the teachers. Well, here's to us.

Dee Us.

They are about to drink

I know. Could I possibly have a glass of water, do you think?

Justin Yes, of course. Look, would everyone like to sit down?

Derek Why not?

Dee Why not? (*To Paige*) Oh, Page Three. I see what you mean. I just got it, yes.

They all sit while Justin fetches some water from the kitchen

Derek We're in garden centres, you know, Micky. All around the Doncaster area. One in Dredsham. One in Pondleton. And another one just outside Clackett.

Paige Oh, yes?

Dee South Yorkshire.

Derek You ever visited Yorkshire? Finest county in the world. Isn't it, Dee?

Dee In the world.

Derek Can't beat it.

Pause

Paige Whereabouts is it, then? Near Birmingham?
Dee Not really, no.

Pause

Derek You can keep Truro, I tell you that.
Dee (*softly*) Don't bring up Truro, love.
Derek No, quite right. Sorry.
Dee We're trying to forget about Truro, aren't we? (*She accepts the water from Justin*) Thank you, Justin. Will we have seen you dancing anywhere, Paige? Have you been in anything we might have seen?
Paige I hope not.
Derek *Cats*? Have you been in *Cats*?
Paige No.
Dee *Phantom of the Opera*?
Paige No.
Derek *Les Misèrables*?
Paige No.
Dee *The Lion King*?
Paige No.
Derek No? That's about the lot, isn't it?
Dee Can't think of any others.
Paige I'm not that sort of dancer.
Dee Oh, I see. You're more...? Are you?
Paige I'm more of a lap dancer——
Justin Classical. Classical dancer. Lapland National Ballet. Famous.
Derek Oh, I see. Classical.
Dee We don't really go for that, do we?
Derek No, can't see what they see in it. (*He pauses slightly*) Trouble with ballet, you can never hear a word they're saying, can you? (*He laughs*)

Dee laughs

Dee No, we prefer it with the songs.
Justin Right.
Dee What about you, Micky? You fond of dancing at all?
Micky No.
Dee Oh.
Paige (*after a slight pause*) Micky prefers the opera.
Derek Right.
Justin (*after a slight pause*) Now then! Anyone ready for a refill?

Derek Not quite yet.
Paige Yes, please.
Justin Yes. (*He reluctantly accepts Paige's empty glass*) The same again?
Paige Same again. Less ice.

Justin refills Paige's glass. Slight pause. The conversation has flagged somewhat

Dee Yes. This is a lovely flat.
Derek Lovely.

Pause. Justin gives Paige her glass and sits in silence

  Ficus elastica variegata.
Paige Pardon?
Derek That plant by the desk. *Ficus elastica variegata.* Or commonly, variegated rubber plant.
Paige Really?
Dee He can do that with everything.

Slight pause

Derek *Dracaena fragrans.* That one by the door.
Justin I wondered what it was.
Dee He's encyclopaedic.

Slight pause

Derek And by the sofa. *Cordyline terminalis.* Needs re-potting, incidentally. Ask me another.
Paige (*softly*) Bloody hell!
Derek Sorry?

The doorbell rings

Dee Is this her? This must be her.
Justin Yes, I'll——
Derek Tell you what, shall we both hide? Both hide, shall we?
Dee Oh, yes. Give Apple a surprise.
Derek Come on, we'll hide in the kitchen.
Dee In the kitchen.

The Jobsons both retreat to the kitchen. Justin waits

Oh, something smells good.
Derek Let her in, then.
Dee Let her in, Justin.
Derek Watch her face.
Dee Can't wait.

Justin gets the key from Micky and opens the front door

Julie-Ann enters. She is wearing a dress from Paige's wardrobe. It is very tight and very revealing and no doubt something that Paige would feel totally at ease in. However, Julie-Ann is evidently acutely self-conscious at the unaccustomed exposure

Julie-Ann (*going straight to Paige*) For heaven's sake, don't you own even one decent dress? Just one that leaves something to the imagination!

Derek and Dee choose this moment to leap out

Derek ⎱
Dee　⎰ (*together*) Surprise!

They stop as they see Julie-Ann. They gape. A brief silence

Julie-Ann (*sheepishly, trying vainly to cover herself*) Hallo, Mummy. Hallo, Daddy.
Dee (*disapprovingly*) Oh! Oh, Apple.
Derek (*likewise*) Oh, dear.
Julie-Ann I'll—er … I'll just fetch a jumper. It's a little chilly.

Julie-Ann hurries off to the bedroom

Dee Well.
Derek Well. That's not our Apple, is it?
Dee It certainly isn't. That's not good, is it?
Derek That's—well, I have to say it—that's bordering on common.
Dee Not like her. Not like Apple, at all. What do you think, Justin?
Derek What's your feeling about it, Justin? You approve of that, do you?
Justin I—I… (*He swallows*) I think she looks sensational.
Derek I see. If she tried wearing something like that when she lived at home she'd be straight to her room with no supper. I mean, I have to say it, a girl wears a dress like that, she's just cheapening herself, in my view.
Paige That's an exclusive designer dress, if you don't mind. And it was certainly not cheap.

Dee Well, I'm sorry, I'm sure we meant no——
Paige It certainly cost a bloody sight more than your off-the-peg Debenhams.
Dee I'm sorry. I see no reason to start attacking——
Derek Hey! Hey! Hey! That's enough of that. Simmer down, girls. Come
   along! Come along! (*He winks at Justin*) Girls and their dresses, eh?
Paige Oh, go and re-pot yourself.
Derek Sorry?
Justin Derek, another whisky?
Derek Not just at present, thank you, Justin. (*To Paige*) Moderation in all
   things.
Paige (*glaring at him*) I'll have another.
Justin No, you won't.

The doorbell rings

Ah, that will either be our main course. Or my mother and her guest. Her
guest is called Olaf—apparently. I'm not quite sure what he does but he's
from Sweden. At least I think it's Sweden. Excuse me a minute.

*Justin goes to the door and admits his mother, Arabella Lazenby. She's
already the worse for wear from drink but like many alcoholics, carries it
off with a certain aplomb. Indeed, she is still good-looking and extremely
stylish*

Paige meanwhile marches to the bar and pours herself another large gin

Arabella (*embracing Justin*) Darling, hallo! Justin, how are you, darling?
Justin Hallo, Mother, I'm very well, thank you. Where's Olaf?
Arabella Olaf I left in the Strand. He is a completely useless Swedish fart,
   darling. If I told him once, I told him ten times… Olaf, drive on the bloody
   left. But he was so drunk by then I don't think he could tell his left from
   his right even in Swedish. So I left him to it and took a taxi. I said to him,
   Olaf, you sort it out with the bus crew, dear. I'm going to see my darling
   boy and his gorgeous new girlfriend. Now let me see her, let me look at her.
   Where is she, then? Where's your little *poule de luxe*? (*She catches sight
   of Paige*) Oh God, Justin, she is *gorgeous*. Thank God! This time she is.
   She's simply *gorgeous*! You clever boy, where did you find this one? She's
   stunning. Hallo, I'm Arabella Lazenby. I'm Justin's mother. I'm so thrilled
   to meet——
Justin (*vainly*) No, Mother, that isn't——
Paige Listen, I'm not——

*Paige is all but smothered by Arabella's embrace. Micky re-locks the front
door during the following*

Arabella My dear, darling girl. I tell you, you are a sight for sore eyes. I
cannot tell you how I was secretly dreading this meeting. (*Still clasping
Paige, she beams round the rest of the assembly*)

*Julie-Ann enters under the following. She has managed to conceal the
more revealing parts of Paige's dress. She has achieved this by wearing
one of Justin's striped football shirts over the top. She has cinched this in
at the waist with one of his ties. Beneath this, the very short skirt peeks
somewhat incongruously*

(*Not seeing Julie-Ann*) Hallo! Whoever you all are! You must be the
Lobsons. Hallo! Well, let me tell you, all of you, this boy of mine, his usual
taste in girls is simply sub-Crufts. I mean, he must pick them up at the
Battersea Dogs Home. They have all been without exception completely
bizarre, bordering on the downright grotesque...

Justin (*quietly at first, under her*) Mother... Mother... Mother...

Arabella (*oblivious*) ...no style, no beauty and certainly not a scrap of sex
appeal. Now suddenly, he's struck pure gold. My darling, I cannot tell you
how welcome you are. The sooner you join this family, the better.

Justin (*loudly*) MOTHER!

Arabella What?

Justin That is Paige who lives upstairs. That is not Julie-Ann.

Arabella It isn't?

Justin That is Julie-Ann.

Dee (*with pride*) That's Julie-Ann.

Derek (*likewise*) Julie-Ann.

Arabella (*gazing at Julie-Ann with some horror*) Oh, my God! He's done
it again. It's another bloody dog!

Julie-Ann bursts into tears and rushes back into the bedroom

Derek (*following after her, concerned*) Julie-Ann...

Dee Julie-Ann...

Derek Apple...

Dee Apple...

The Jobsons go after their daughter

Arabella What did I say? Did I say something?

Justin Thank you so much, Mother...

Arabella Sorry, darling. I think I'm suffering from the effects of my car
crash. I badly need to lie down for a minute... (*Her knees suddenly give
way*)

Paige Catch her!

Micky and Justin react swiftly but fail to save Arabella, who nonetheless collapses conveniently on the sofa. Silence. From the bedroom, the sounds of loud wailing from Julie-Ann

Justin (*at last, cheerfully*) Well. Happy times. Anyone for soup?

Micky and Paige stare at him. As Justin returns to the kitchen, the Lights fade to Black-out

CURTAIN

ACT II

The same. Two hours later. It has stopped raining at last

Arabella is asleep on the sofa, having slept through the entire meal, which is now nearing its end. She occasionally snores softly. Sounds of voices from the distant dining room. Loud laughter from the three Jobsons

In a moment, Julie-Ann enters with a cup of coffee. She is now wearing her original dress and seems more cheerful. Evidently she and Paige have done a clothes swap. Julie-Ann goes over to Arabella and hesitates a second. She then starts gently to try to shake her awake

Julie-Ann Mrs Lazenby… Mrs Lazenby…

Arabella suddenly wakes with a snort, startling Julie-Ann

Arabella Wahh-hah-waaah! Who? Who did you say?

Julie-Ann Mrs Lazenby…

Arabella Where am I? Who the hell are you?

Julie-Ann I'm Julie-Ann, Mrs Lazenby. Justin's—girlfriend.

Arabella Oh, God. So you are. Hallo, there. I thought for a minute you were that other frightful thing in a football shirt.

Julie-Ann Yes, that was me, Mrs Lazenby…

Arabella Looked liked a Welsh pug, didn't she? Is that coffee intended for me?

Julie-Ann Yes, I thought you might…

Arabella No, thank you. I never drink coffee, it's very, very bad for me, it keeps me awake for days. If you have such a thing as a small brandy, I'd be most awfully grateful.

Julie-Ann (*uncertainly*) Brandy. Yes…

Arabella Thank you so much. Just the merest dribble.

Julie-Ann Yes. (*She puts the coffee cup down on the table and goes to the bar, where she pours a modest brandy*)

Arabella Have I been asleep?

Julie-Ann Yes.

Arabella Good Lord. How long for?

Julie-Ann Two hours. We've all had dinner. Would you care for something to eat?

Arabella No, thank you. I never eat at this time of night. It's terribly bad for me. What time is it?

Julie-Ann Just after nine. (*She holds up the brandy glass*) Is that enough?

Arabella Tiddly bit more, darling.

Julie-Ann pours some more and brings it over to Arabella

Julie-Ann You're sure you won't have a little chicken?

Arabella A little what?

Julie-Ann Chicken. To eat.

Arabella Good God, no.

Julie-Ann How about some mousse?

Arabella No, it's very sweet of you, darling, but I can't stand reindeer meat. It's far too rich. I honestly don't know what people see in it. (*She takes the brandy*) Thank you so much. (*She throws back the brandy in one*) That's lovely. Thank you.

Julie-Ann (*sitting and starting to sip the coffee*) I just wanted to say—I think—we may have got off on the wrong foot.

Arabella Foot?

Julie-Ann I realize you were probably still in shock from your accident but I just wanted to say that I hope we can be friends. I'd like us to be friends. After all, we both love Justin, don't we? We have that in common.

Arabella What accident?

Julie-Ann You were in an accident.

Arabella Was I?

Julie-Ann Apparently. In your car. With a bus.

Arabella Good Lord. Was I hurt?

Julie-Ann I don't think so. Just shocked.

Arabella Was I driving?

Julie-Ann No, I think it was a man called Olaf.

Arabella Extraordinary. You know, I've completely forgotten all about it. I do a lot of that these days. Well, Sally-Ann, I'm certain us two, we're going to be absolute bosom buddies... Could you possibly get me another teeny one of these, dear, would you mind?

Julie-Ann Yes, Mrs Lazenby.

Arabella (*flashing her a winning smile*) Arabella.

Julie-Ann Arabella. (*She returns to the bar*) And it's Julie-Ann.

Arabella Is it? It's very, very good whatever it is. I don't think I've tried it before.

Julie-Ann refills the glass and returns it to Arabella

By the way, for God's sake, don't call me Mrs Lazenby. I can't stand being called Mrs Lazenby. I haven't been Mrs Lazenby for years. Not since Lazenby walked out on me in Cairo taking every single traveller's cheque I had. (*She accepts the glass*) Thank you so much. (*She drinks*) Lovely. What did you say it was called. Julie—?

Julie-Ann Julie-Ann. No, that's my name.

Arabella (*rising uncertainly*) Well, good luck to you, darling. Just pray he doesn't take after his bloody father, that's all I can say. (*She lurches towards the door*) I'm just going to powder my nose. It's somewhere through here, I take it? Then I must join the party. See you in a minute, Polly.

Julie-Ann Yes.

Arabella exits

Julie-Ann stands for a moment, frowning. There has been, in her view, a distinct failure to communicate. She goes into the kitchen and pours the rest of the coffee away. There is a bowl in the sink filled with soapy water. They have obviously, to some extent, been washing up as they went along. She rinses the cup and starts to sing

Derek and Justin come in. Derek has his nearly-empty coffee cup

Justin (*as he enters*) ...no, it's leasehold. Long lease. I've been here just over five years.

Derek It's well positioned...

Justin Yes, it's very handy for my work and the area's still developing all the time. Well, all around Docklands, of course...

They see Julie-Ann

Derek Hallo, Apple.

Julie-Ann Hallo, Daddy. Everything all right?

Derek Absolutely perfect. Beautiful meal, Apple, first class.

Julie-Ann Thank you. Justin did the soup. I did the Kiwi Mousse——

Derek Wonderful. Er—would you—would you give us a couple of minutes alone, Apple? Would you mind?

Julie-Ann What? (*She realizes*) Oh, yes. Of course. (*She starts to go out hurriedly*)

Derek Just a couple of minutes, darling.

Julie-Ann (*leaving*) Of course...

Julie-Ann goes off to the dining-room

Derek Temperament like an angel, hasn't she?

Justin Oh, yes.

Derek Just like her mother.

Justin Right.

Derek Do you find that?

Justin Well, of course, I've only just met her mother...

Derek She and I, we haven't exchanged a word in anger in twenty-three years.

Justin You and Julie-Ann?

Derek Me and Dee. Few couples can say that.

Justin Very few.

Derek Aha! Do I spy brandy?

Justin Yes, would you like a——

Derek Wouldn't say no.

Justin pours them both a brandy at the bar during the following. Derek moves in on him

Now, Justin, I wanted a quick word.

Justin Yes?

Derek I don't want to pre-empt anything you're maybe going to announce this evening—frankly, we have had wind that there might be a speech in the offing and I don't want to anticipate that in any way—but I'd like you to be filled in on the situation as it stands—in regard to our own standpoint. Mine and Dee's. Number one, we're over the moon about you and Julie-Ann, we really are.

Justin Thank you.

Derek We knew we'd take to you. She kept us posted about you, of course. We liked the sound of you, Justin, and we're not disappointed.

Justin I'm glad.

Derek To be honest, between these four walls, we've had a lot of heartbreak with our other two girls. But this time, I think we've made it. (*He takes the brandy at last*) Thank you. Good health.

Justin Good health.

Derek Right, very briefly, Jobson's—that's my firm—consists of three separate garden centres. All near Doncaster. One in Dredsham. One in Pondleton. And the other one just outside Clackett. All of them prime sites, all in South Yorkshire. Now, you won't believe this, Justin, nobody does. But I'm nearly sixty. You wouldn't believe that now, would you?

Justin (*trying to sound amazed*) Goodness, no.

Derek Nonetheless, it's time for me to be looking ahead, Justin. You know what they say. There is no such thing in life as immortality. Not in this life, anyway. So. To put it bluntly, I'm looking for a son and heir, Justin. Someone to take up the Jobson's banner. Yes? You with me so far?

Justin Ah. Well, I'm——
Derek No, you don't have to say anything. Not at this stage. I'm dropping
that in your ear, that's all I'm doing. In your ear. Once you've had time to
think, you must come north and see for yourself. I think you'll be
impressed, Justin, I think you'll be excited. I know you will. I think you'll
feel the tingle of challenge, lad. Hear what I'm saying?
Justin Yes, well, of course I'd love to come and look round but I'm not sure
it's my sort of thing really. Garden centres. I mean, my line is computers.
Derek Justin, can I say this? May I simply say, I'll be the judge of that? Hear
what I'm saying? Justin, I'm saying I know that, in my water, you're a
garden-centre man. All right? I can feel it, Justin.
Justin (*rather alarmed*) Can you?

Paige and Micky enter. Micky is on his mobile. Paige is fairly drunk

Micky (*coming on, into the mobile*) ...yes ... no... OK, Winston ... yes...
Derek Would you mind, for a second? We're just having a private word here.

*Micky ignores them and opens the balcony windows and steps outside,
pushing Paige ahead of him*

Micky (*as he does so*) ...yes ... no... OK ... yes, Winston...
Paige (*to the others*) Excuse us.

Micky closes the doors and we can no longer hear the phone call

Derek I have to say I'm not altogether struck with the quality of your
neighbours, Justin.
Justin No?
Derek But then that's London for you. Have you known them long?
Justin No. No time at all.
Derek I mean, they seem very devoted to each other, almost inseparable—
I approve of that—I mean, they even go to the toilet together, don't they?
Have you noticed?
Justin Well...
Derek No, but that little girl, she's got a tongue on her. Never heard language
like it in my life. Not from a woman. Effing and blinding. Pass the effing
this. I mean, frankly, I don't see the need for it, Justin. And it's everywhere,
isn't it? Have you noticed? Television, newspapers. Films. We can't go
any more, Dee and me. To the cinema. Last film we saw was *Sound of
Music*. I mean, face it, all this sex everywhere you turn. Who needs it? I
certainly don't. Do you want it? Thrust in your face, practically rammed
down your throat every place you turn? 'Course you don't. Ordinary

people—you, me, Dee, Julie-Ann. We can do without all that, thank you very much.

Justin (*faintly*) Yes...

Micky and Paige come in from the balcony, leaving the windows open. Micky has finished the phone call. They are arguing

Micky ...listen, I'm just doing what I'm paid for, that's all...

Paige ...come on, Micky, don't give me all that shit, you bastard...

Micky ...there's no point in arguing, Paige, I do what I'm told, that's all...

Paige Well, fuck you...

Paige and Micky go off towards the dining-room

Derek Wants her mouth rinsing out with washing-up liquid, that one. That's what we did with our eldest, Lucy-Jane. She never swore again, I tell you that. Sick for days.

Justin (*closing the windows again*) Yes. Derek, how about your other two daughters? Aren't they interested in taking over? Possibly?

Derek Listen. This is to go no further than these walls because it upsets my wife. Our eldest, Lucy-Jane—she has—how shall I put it—selected an unnatural alternative lifestyle. One that her mother and I cannot countenance.

Justin An alternative—? You mean she's joined some sect?

Derek In a way. (*He finds this difficult*) In a phrase, she's gone to Canada. With a female friend. And turned her back on conventional sexual behaviour.

Justin Oh, I see. Well.

Derek I don't need to spell it out. She's formed an unnatural relationship and broken her mother's heart, Justin. She was set on grandchildren, you see. We both were.

Justin But surely she's still your daughter?

Derek Not any more. I think it's all down to you and Julie-Ann now, Justin. I said to Dee, thank God there's one.

Justin How about your other daughter? She's married, isn't she?

Derek Sally-Jo? Yes, she's married.

Justin But no children?

Derek (*grimly*) Four children.

Justin Well, then.

Derek But—it's not a marriage we can countenance, Justin.

Justin Why on earth not?

Derek He's—he's a ... nice enough lad but... He's... I sincerely believe, Justin, that human beings are like garden fish.

Justin Sorry?

Derek We were made different colours for a good reason, Justin. To differentiate us. So you don't get a goldfish spawning with a rainbow carp, you follow what I'm saying?

Justin (*bewildered*) No...

Derek I've nothing against any man. Live and let live. Evil unto no-one. But each in his own ornamental pond, Justin. That's all I'm saying.

Justin I don't quite follow this. Are you saying your son-in-law is black?

Derek He's Chinese.

Justin (*shaking his head*) My God!

Derek So you understand?

Justin Excuse me, I just have to—I just have to go—out here—for a minute... Excuse me.

Derek Think it over, what I said, won't you?

Justin Yes. My God!

Justin passes Arabella in the doorway with her empty glass

Derek seems pleased with himself. He walks to the window and looks out

Arabella (*to Justin*) Hallo, darling. May I help myself...

Justin (*on his way out*) Please do, Mother.

Justin goes out to the dining-room

Arabella (*seeing Derek*) Hallo, there.

Derek Hallo, there.

Arabella Mr Dobson...

Derek Jobson, yes.

Arabella (*helping herself to another brandy*) I've just been talking to your jolly wife. She's an absolute hoot, isn't she? She was telling me all about your shops.

Derek Garden centres, yes.

Arabella They sound quite extraordinary.

Derek Well, you must come and have a look round. You'd be most welcome any time. I'll give you a special conducted tour.

Arabella But aren't they in Yorkshire?

Derek That's right.

Arabella That's a hell of a long way to look at a load of bloody garden gnomes, isn't it?

Derek (*put out*) Well, we do sell a good deal more than that.

Arabella Actually, if you don't mind my saying so, you do look a little bit like a garden gnome yourself. Has anyone ever told you?

Derek (*moving away*) Excuse me. Just check how they're getting on in there.

Arabella Jolly good, you do that. (*She sips her brandy and eventually sits*)

Derek heads for the door. He steps aside to let first Dee, then Julie-Ann, then Paige and Micky, and finally Justin pass. Justin and the women all carry dirty plates and cutlery. Micky is empty-handed

Dee (*passing Derek*) We're all just coming through, dear.
Derek Good. Good. Won't be a minute.

Derek goes out

Julie-Ann (*to Paige*) Just put them on here...
Dee (*calling after Derek*) Could you bring some things through when you come, dear?
Derek (*off*) What?
Dee (*calling*) Could you bring some things through?

Derek returns

Derek What was that?
Dee Could you bring some things through?
Derek Oh, right. I'm just going to the—you-know-where. You don't have to come with me, though. (*He laughs*)

Dee laughs

Derek goes out again

Paige and Micky have gone through to the sitting-room. They sit. Micky looks at his watch. Julie-Ann is tidying away. Justin takes the plates from Dee and stacks them ready for washing

Dee Now leave all this to me, Apple.
Julie-Ann No, we won't do it now, Mummy.
Dee Won't take a minute. We can't leave it all for Justin, can we?
Julie-Ann We don't need to do it now.
Dee Won't take a second, Apple. Don't sulk.
Julie-Ann Really...

Julie-Ann goes out to the dining-room again

Arabella (*to Paige and Micky*) Hallo, there.
Paige Hallo.

Micky nods

Arabella It's the Siamese twins.

Dee starts washing up. As she does so she starts singing discordantly, very much like Julie-Ann did. Justin stares at her in horror

Dee (*to Justin*) What you need is a dishwasher.
Justin Yes. Of course, generally there's only the two of me. One of me.
Derek (*off, calling inaudibly*) Grob de luxe in fender.

Justin watches the following with appalled fascination

Dee (*calling*) What's that, dear?
Derek (*off, calling inaudibly*) Grob de luxe in fender.
Dee Excuse me. (*She moves off, calling*) I can't hear you, dear. What did you say?

Dee goes out

Justin starts on the washing-up

Arabella (*intimately, to Paige*) I'm awfully glad he's marrying you, you know.
Paige What?
Arabella Rather than that other one.
Paige Who's marrying who?
Arabella My son.
Paige Yes?
Arabella Marrying you.
Paige No, he's not.
Arabella My God, you haven't broken it off already, have you? They all do that in the end, you know. None of them can put up with him for more than ten minutes.
Paige No, he's marrying the other one.
Arabella What other one?
Justin (*pained, listening to this from the kitchen*) Mother!
Arabella Well, I don't know, you all look alike to me. So long as it's not the one in the football jersey... (*To Micky*) And what are you both doing here?
Paige We're neighbours.
Arabella Neighbours?
Paige From upstairs.
Arabella I see. I'm his mother.
Paige Yes.
Arabella What do you do?

Paige I've retired. I used to be a dancer.

Arabella A dancer! How super! Yes, I can see you. Have you danced *Coppélia*? You must have danced *Coppélia*, surely?

Paige No, I've only been as far as Amsterdam.

Arabella (*only a little mystified*) Yes? I'm afraid I missed that. (*To Micky*) And you? How about you?

Paige Micky's in security.

Arabella Security? Do you drive around in a van with a plastic hat on, then?

Micky What?

Paige He used to be a boxer.

Arabella A boxer? Oh, terrific! I adore boxing. I'm a great fan. I find it riveting.

Micky Do you?

Arabella Oh, yes. My second husband used to take me to live fights all the time. Before he left me. Desperately exciting. I adore the atmosphere.

Micky Can't beat it.

Arabella It must have been fantastic being in the actual ring itself, wasn't it?

Micky Er—sometimes.

Arabella Wasn't it exciting for you? It must have been thrilling, surely?

Micky Yes. From what I can remember. I mean, there was usually someone in there with you trying to flatten you, of course.

Arabella Oh, to be a man! I'd love to have had a go. Were you successful? I mean, did you win a lot of fights?

Micky (*unhappily*) I—er... Well, I... (*He hesitates. He looks at Paige*)

Arabella does likewise

Paige He was brillantly successful.

Arabella Really? What made you give up? (*She looks at Paige again*)

Paige Micky had a rare medical condition. He retired undefeated. Didn't you?

Micky I—er...

Paige He's still got his belt.

Arabella How impressive.

Dee comes back with more items from the dining room. Cruets, mats, etc. Julie-Ann follows, returning the kitchen chairs to their original places

Dee Nearly there. Just the glasses. And odds and ends.

Arabella Listen, I really must lend them a hand. Do my bit. Will you excuse me?

Paige Certainly.

Dee goes out again. Arabella follows

Julie-Ann fusses in the kitchen for a second. Justin continues to wash dishes.
Micky gets up

Micky I don't know what to do, Paige. I don't know what to do for the best.
Paige I've told you, it's your call, Micky. All I can say is that if I'm here when
Rudy gets back, I'm as good as dead, aren't I?
Micky But if you're not here when he comes back, then I'm certainly dead.
Paige What did Winston say to you?
Micky Two of our lads didn't even go the distance and Rudy wasn't in a very
good mood...
Paige Bloody hell! God help us both.

Julie-Ann has come out of the kitchen and moves to Paige. She speaks over
Paige's next

Then all I can say is we might as well open those bloody windows here and
now and jump in that river——
Julie-Ann (*simultaneously*) I would be extremely grateful if for the
remainder of this evening you would mind moderating your language in
front of my parents.
Paige (*sourly*) Oh, sod off, you stupid cow.

Julie-Ann tosses her head contemptuously and exits

Micky (*unhappily*) I don't know what to do, Paige.
Paige (*rising, angrily*) Well, you're going to have to make a decision soon,
aren't you, Micky? Because I don't want to die even if you do.

Justin has come through from the kitchen in response to her raised voice

(*Apologetically*) Sorry, Justin. Buggering up your evening, aren't we?
Justin You OK?
Paige We'll try and behave ourselves. While we're here. It's just that they're
not our sort of people, these, really.
Justin I'm—I'm not at all surprised. As a matter of fact they're not——

A loud crash of breaking glass interrupts him. A scream from Dee. Paige and
Micky rise startled. Micky produces his gun

Arabella (*off*) Oh, shit!
Justin (*hurrying to the door*) Oh, Mother...

Paige What the hell was that?

Consternation off from Dee and Julie-Ann

Justin Mother...

Justin dashes off

Paige Micky, put the gun away.

Micky does so

It's not even loaded, is it?
Micky How do you know?
Paige Because Rudy's got more sense than to trust you with a loaded gun, that's why. Probably blow your foot off. Or his.
Micky Don't tell anyone, will you?
Paige Wouldn't dream of it.
Micky I could lose—credibility.

Julie-Ann dashes on briefly. She grabs a dustpan and brush from under the sink and hurries off again

Shortly, the sound of glass being swept up offstage and more voices

Why'd you tell that woman I was a champion boxer?
Paige (*shrugging*) I don't know. Didn't want you to lose your credibility, I suppose.

Arabella is helped on, supported by Derek and Julie-Ann

Derek ...carefully, carefully, mind yourself here...
Arabella ...so silly of me ... sheer carelessness... I was thinking of something else... I'm so frightfully sorry...
Julie-Ann So long as you're all right...
Arabella Oh, I'm perfectly fine, don't worry... Your poor glasses.

They reach the armchair

Derek Here we are. Sit her here. Sit her down here.

Arabella is lowered into it by Julie-Ann and Derek

(*To the others*) She just had a little topple, that's all.

Arabella I didn't topple. It's that bloody silly carpet.

Julie-Ann There isn't a carpet.

Arabella Well, there should have been a carpet, shouldn't there?

Derek Never mind, never mind. No bones broken.

Julie-Ann Just fourteen glasses.

Derek Doesn't matter, Apple, doesn't matter. Shall we all sit down, shall we? Yes. Before we do any more damage.

Derek sits in the desk chair. Julie-Ann sits on the sofa. Paige sits on a bar stool. Micky continues to stand near the front door. Silence

Dee enters

Dee (*softly*) I've just brushed it all into a little pile, Apple. Better wrap it in lots of newspaper before you throw it away.

Julie-Ann Right.

Dee Otherwise you might cut the dustman.

Julie-Ann Yes.

Dee sits on the sofa next to Julie-Ann. She has no sooner sat down than she gives a cry and springs up again

Derek What's the matter?

Dee produces a dessert fork from the cushions

Dee Sat on a fork. How did that get there?

Julie-Ann (*drily*) Heaven knows.

Pause. Arabella appears to be dozing again

Dee Justin's trying to get her a—(*mouthing*)—taxi——

Arabella (*opening her eyes*) Get me a what?

Dee A taxi.

Arabella That'll cost a fortune.

Dee He thinks you should be home in your bed.

Arabella All the way to Godalming? I could buy a yacht for that.

Dee Moor up outside the window then, couldn't you?

Derek Then you can watch your son go over the yardarm. (*He laughs*)

Dee and Julie-Ann laugh with him. The others stare at them

Justin returns, unseen by everyone but Paige. He stares

Dee (*drying her eyes*) Son go over the yardarm. I like that. That's very good.

Silence

Arabella What the hell is a yardarm, anyway? Anybody know?
Derek It's when your fingers dangle down below your knees... (*He laughs*)
Dee (*laughing*) ...below your knees...
Julie-Ann (*laughing, identically*) ...below your knees...

The others stare at them. Silence

Arabella I think I must be missing all these, you know. I don't quite get them.

The others notice that Paige is staring at Justin

Oh, hallo, darling. Come in and join in the fun. We're all laughing our heads off.
Justin I've got you a taxi coming, Mother. Found one that's agreed to take you.
Derek Sit down for a minute, Justin. Pull up a chair.
Justin Right.
Derek We can all sit together for a minute, anyway.
Dee Oh, yes.

Justin starts to bring a kitchen chair through to the sitting-room. He sees Micky is still standing

Justin Micky?
Micky What?
Justin A chair?
Micky No, it's OK, I'm——
Justin Come on, there's two here.

Micky takes the chair sooner than argue. He sits near the front door. Justin brings the other chair through and sits in the kitchen doorway. They are now all assembled. Silence

Well. What's new?

Pause

Julie-Ann My mother just sat on a fork.
Justin Really?

Julie-Ann A dessert fork.
Justin Ah.

Pause

Derek Here's one. You won't have heard this. It's a good 'un.
Dee He's going to tell a joke.
Julie-Ann Are you going to tell us a joke, Dad?
Dee He knows millions of jokes.
Derek There's these three fellers, one of them's Jewish, one of them's a
    Pakistani and the other one's queer...
Arabella You know I simply adore your accent, I'm absolutely riveted by
    it. It's like listening to gravy. Rich, thick gravy.
Derek Beg your pardon?
Arabella Whereas hers is completely different. (*She indicates Paige*) Your
    daughter's accent here is from the other end of the country entirely. How
    do you explain that?
Derek That's not my daughter.
Arabella Isn't she?
Dee (*indicating Julie-Ann*) This is our daughter.
Arabella Oh, that's your daughter. I wish you'd make up your bloody mind.
Justin We keep telling you, Mother.
Arabella (*muttering*) Well, they both look identical to me. I don't know how
    you're ever supposed to tell them apart.
Julie-Ann (*murmuring*) I sincerely hope you can.

Silence

Paige (*suddenly*) I didn't always talk like this. I used to talk very, very posh
    indeed because I come originally from this amazingly smart family. They
    were real upper class. Only when I was sixteen, see, I was riding on the back
    of my boyfriend's motorbike only we weren't wearing helmets and we hit
    this hole in the road doing about seventy-five and we were both hurled sixty
    feet into a brick wall and he was killed outright and I was in a coma for
    eighteen months.
Dee Oh, dear.
Derek Dear.
Paige And when I finally came to, my memory was completely gone. My
    head was totally empty. I didn't know who I was or anything. They told me
    I was like a child of two. And I had to be taught everything, all over again.
    How to talk, how to write, how to feed myself. I even had to learn how to
    go to the toilet. And I had this one nurse that taught me everything, you see.
    Everything. Only she talked like this. So subsequently when I learnt to talk

again, I talked like her. Like this. Only if she'd been Welsh or Scottish, I'd
probably have had a Taffy accent, you see. Or Scotch.

Silence

I never told anyone that before.
Julie-Ann (*softly*) I'm not surprised.
Paige Thought you might be interested.
Julie-Ann (*sotto voce*) Justy...
Justin Mmm?
Julie-Ann Are you going to...?
Justin Mmm?
Julie-Ann Speech.
Justin What?
Julie-Ann (*a little louder*) Speech.
Justin Yes.

A silence

Arabella Has anyone been to Glyndebourne this year?

Silence

No? Well, you missed nothing, I can tell you that. I only went for the
Mozart. It was the worst *Flute* I've ever had the misfortune to hear.
Derek Really?
Arabella Dreadful.

Slight pause

Dee What was the rest of the orchestra like?
Arabella I beg your pardon?

Silence

Julie-Ann (*sotto voce*) Justy... Speech. Make your speech.
Justin Ah...
Derek This one you'll like. There's this West Indian bookie and he's trying
   to——
Julie-Ann Daddy, I'm sorry to interrupt. I think Justin has something to say
   to us all. Speech!
Derek Oh, I'm sorry. Has he? Justin. Speech!
Dee Speech!

Julie-Ann Speech!

Justin Yes. (*He rises*) Yes. Er... Derek... Dee... Mother... Er... Yes. I wanted to say. I have something I need to say to you all. It's with... It's with great...

Julie-Ann (*encouragingly*) Go on, Justy, we're all listening, darling...

Justin It's with ... it's ... it's... (*Suddenly he bursts loudly into song*)

It's a long way to Tipperary,
It's a long way to go;
It's a long way to Tipperary,
And the sweetest girl I know.
Goodbye Piccadilly,
Farewell Leicester Square:
It's a long, long way to Tipperary,
But my heart's right there.

He finishes and sits down. A stunned silence

Arabella (*applauding, finally*) Jolly good, darling!

Julie-Ann Justy!

Micky's mobile rings. Both he and Paige jump slightly

Micky Excuse me. (*He moves to the front door*)

Arabella speaks under the following

(*Into the phone, sotto voce*) Yes ... yes ... sure, Rudy ... yes ... OK. Yes, Rudy.

Arabella (*simultaneously*) Has anybody else got a turn they can do? (*To Julie-Ann*) Weren't you telling me you were a dancer?

Paige No, that was me.

Arabella You? Well, how about a dance, then?

Justin I don't think so, Mother.

Micky has finished his phone call. Paige is looking at him

Micky They're on their way back. They'll be here in just under an hour.

Paige Right.

Dee Expecting friends, are you?

Paige No.

Silence. Paige suddenly springs off her stool. There is a desperation about her

All right. Here we go then. You want a dance, I'll give you a dance, then.
Justin Paige...
Paige I'll give you a dance you won't forget, you bastards.
Arabella Oh, lovely.
Paige (*moving to the CD player*) This thing work, does it?
Julie-Ann What do you think you're doing?

Paige starts to sifts through the CDs. Carelessly tossing them aside until she finds one she likes

Justin Paige...
Paige Here! This'll do! (*She switches on the player and loads the CD*) Ready then. Here we go! (*She presses the remote play*)

A raunchy tune starts up and Paige goes into her routine. Hardly subtle and, in the context of the occasion, somewhat indelicate. Although she makes passing contact with both Derek and Micky it is towards Justin that she directs most of her lap-dancing expertise. The sequence is short and steamy. The party sit transfixed until Julie-Ann, unable to contain herself a moment longer, hurls herself in a fury first to switch off the CD player and then at Paige herself. Paige, temporarily taken off-balance, soon recovers. She is an experienced street fighter, more than a match for Julie-Ann. The two grapple for a moment until the others finally intervene. Micky drags Paige clear, pinioning her arms to her side. Paige continues to snarl, kick and struggle in his grasp like a wild animal. Julie-Ann, rescued by Dee and Derek, is hysterical with anger and frustration. All the following overlaps

Justin Julie, for God's sake ... what do you think you're doing... Paige... Come on, that'll do. Someone's going to get hurt in a minute, come on... (*Etc.*)
Micky (*simultaneously*) Oy! Oy! That's it! That's enough of that! Paige! You're out of order, Paige, out of order! Come on, calm down... (*Etc.*)
Derek (*simultaneously*) Now then, girls. Now then, girls. Julie-Ann, you stop that at once. Apple, come on. Control, Apple ... control... Apple... Apple... Apple... (*Etc.*)
Dee (*simultaneously*) Julie-Ann, stop that ... stop it, stop it, stop it! She's not worth it, the little slut... Don't you hurt my daughter, young woman. How dare you... (*Etc.*)
Arabella (*simultaneously*) Oh, things are hotting up, aren't they? All we need is a spot of mud and we'll have the full cabaret. I'm putting my money on the blonde. Five to one the blonde, fifteen to one the brunette... (*Etc.*)

Till finally:

Derek (*to Dee, whilst restraining Julie-Ann*) Bring her in the bedroom, take
her in the bedroom, Dee...
Dee Right. Come along, Apple, come along, darling. Calm down. (*To Paige,
as she goes*) You vicious, brazen little hussy...

Derek and Dee go off with Julie-Ann to the bedroom

*Paige has exhausted herself from her struggles. Micky puts her firmly in the
armchair*

Micky You sit there and calm down. You get up again, I will knock you down
in person. All right?

*Paige doesn't move but buries her head in her hands and remains motionless
during the following. Justin surveys the scene with incredulity*

Justin (*softly*) Good God!
Arabella Is it all over, then?
Justin Yes, Mother.

The doorbell rings. Paige and Micky look up

Micky (*to Paige*) Can't be them. Not yet.
Justin Might be the cab. Just a minute. (*He retrieves the key from Micky once
again*)

Justin goes out of the front door briefly

Arabella Did he say that was my taxi?
Micky Possibly.
Arabella Splendid. (*She starts to get up*)

Justin returns

Justin Yes, it's the cab. You ready, Mother?
Arabella Yes, I think I've got everything... Thank you for a lovely evening,
darling. Absolutely fabulous. (*To Paige*) And lovely to meet you and I do
hope to see a lot more of you in the future. You must come to Godalming.
It's absolutely beautiful.
Justin Come on, Mother. Is this your coat?
Arabella Yes, it could be. Looks rather like it.
Justin Right. Off we go then. He's waiting——
Arabella Well, he can bloody well wait, darling. He's only a cab driver, for

God's sake. (*To Micky*) Goodnight. I wish I'd seen you box, you know. I'm sure she's right. You must have been terrific. 'Bye.
Micky 'Bye.

Arabella goes out with Justin

Paige and Micky are alone again. A silence. Micky sits, a troubled man. Quite suddenly, still in the armchair, Paige starts to scream and drum her arms and legs in a frenzy of anger, frustration and despair. The cry of someone who senses their meaningless, wasted life is all but over. She rips off her jewellery and hurls it across the room. This attack continues for some time. Micky stares at her but does not move. Just as suddenly, Paige stops. Silence

Paige (*recovering, dully*) So what's the score now, Micky?
Micky (*unhappily*) Same as ever. Wait for Rudy.
Paige Just checking.
Micky It's the only way, Paige. I can't see another way.
Paige Micky, you would be stuck for choice at a crossroads, you would. All right. We'd better go upstairs and wait then, hadn't we?
Micky Upstairs?
Paige Well, we don't want to involve these people, do we now? And if Rudy has to come down here for me, then, like it or not, they will be seriously involved.
Micky See what you mean. They'll be forty minutes yet. Winston's driving. You know he don't like overtaking.
Paige Right. Comes of driving a hearse all those years.

Justin enters

Micky re-locks the door

Justin I hope Mother'll be all right. It's a mini-cab and he doesn't seem to speak much English. Ah, well...
Paige We'll be going upstairs in a minute, Justin. Leave you in peace.
Justin Upstairs, but...
Paige Thank you so much. I know we must have wrecked your evening completely and I really do apologise for roughing up your girlfriend, but she had it coming, Justin, she really did, I'm sorry. Someone had to do it.
Justin Probably. I don't know.

Dee appears in the doorway. She has the manner of someone attending a funeral

(*Seeing her*) Oh. How is she?

Dee Justin, she would like a private word with you, please.
Justin (*alarmed by Dee's manner*) She's all right, isn't she?
Dee If you could step this way a moment.
Justin Yes, right, I'll...

Julie-Ann appears in the doorway behind her mother. She is pale and shaky but otherwise unharmed

Julie-Ann It's all right, Mummy...
Dee Apple, what are you doing standing up, Apple?
Julie-Ann I'm all right.
Dee You should be lying down.
Julie-Ann Would you leave us a moment, please? I'd just like a private word with Justin.
Dee But surely we should be here to keep an eye on you, darling. You're so weak, you can hardly...
Julie-Ann Please! All of you. Leave us! Please!
Paige Yes, well, we were going, anyway.
Justin Wait in the dining-room, would you?
Paige No, we might as well——
Justin Please.
Paige OK.

Paige and Micky make to go off together with Dee

Don't be too long.

The three of them leave

Justin Do you need to sit down?
Julie-Ann No. (*She gathers her thoughts*) I just want to say, Justin, that I'm prepared to draw a veil over tonight. I think a lot of things went wrong—and some of it was probably my fault and some of it was yours. And some of it was that woman's for bursting in and ruining our evening. All of us—and I know I'm speaking for my parents—we all want you to be part of our family. And I want to make this work. I love you very much, Justin. And I believe you love me. And I think we could have a happy life together. Given the right circumstances. That's all I have to say.

Silence

You don't have to answer, not this minute. I just wanted to let you know my feelings. I love you very much, Justin. (*Tearfully*) Now, please excuse

me. I have to lie down again for a little. My parents will be running me home soon. I'll leave you to make up your own mind. (*She turns and starts to go off*)
Justin (*calling after her*) Julie——
Julie-Ann (*without looking back*) 'Night.

Julie-Ann exits

Justin stands in an agony of indecision

Justin Oh, God!

The doorbell rings

Who the hell—?

Paige and Micky arrive in the dining-room doorway

Micky It can't be.
Justin (*realizing who it must be*) Oh. It's OK. I'll tell him you're not here. I'll say I've never heard of you...
Micky He's not going to——
Paige Don't be stupid, Justin. It's got nothing to do with—oh, God!
Justin Ssshh!

Micky tosses him the key. Justin marches swiftly to the door and throws it open

Hallo! Can I help you at——

Arabella is standing there. She marches past him and into the flat

Arabella Well, so much for mini-cabs, darling. Not only did it not have a single working seat belt but the dear man hadn't a clue where we were going. He seemed to think, as far as I could gather from his strangled English, that I wanted to go somewhere in EC4. Which is all of a hundred and fifty yards away.
Justin EC4. I told them Godalming.
Arabella Well, he was hell-bent on Godliman Street, EC4. He had no knowledge of Godalming. Or indeed of Surrey. Surrey, I said. I'm very Surrey, he said. Surrey? No, I'm Surrey. We could have been at it all night. Apologising to each other in pidgin Urdu. So here I am again.
Justin I'd better try somewhere else for you. I'll get my address book. They're usually very reliable, that firm.

Justin goes off

Arabella (*to the others*) Hallo, again.
Paige (*dully*) Hallo. (*She sits*)

Arabella waits. A silence

Micky Where is this Godalming, then?
Arabella Surrey. Very close to Guildford. Do you know Guildford?
Micky Oh, yes. I know Guildford. It's near Woking.
Arabella Absolutely right.
Micky Which isn't far from Leatherhead.
Arabella True.
Micky Which is not a stone's throw from Reigate.
Arabella (*tiring of this*) Yes, well, everything's incredibly close these days, isn't it?

Silence

Micky I'll give you a lift, if you like.
Paige What?
Arabella What?
Micky I said I could give you a lift. If you like.
Arabella Oh. Well. (*She pauses slightly*) Do you have a car?
Micky Oh, yes. I've got a car. Downstairs in the garage. Black Mercedes. Top-of-the-range automatic.
Paige Micky...
Micky Fully air-conditioned, latest reg. Smoked glass, bullet-proof windows, ABS braking...
Paige Micky, for God's sake——
Micky Surround-sound stereo, built-in TV-video and a five-line cellular phone system. (*With an afterthought*) And heated wing mirrors.
Arabella (*tempted by the offer*) Well. Does it have working seat belts, though?
Micky Oh, yes. It's got seat belts. Six of them.
Arabella And do you prefer to drive on the left?
Micky All the time.
Arabella Well, in that case, thank you very much. If it's not out of your way.
Micky Not really.
Arabella No?
Micky I don't have a way.

They start to move to the door

(*To Paige*) Coming, then?

Paige Why you doing this, Micky?

Micky I don't know—I thought of you, in that hospital—with that nurse— her spending all that time teaching you and that. And I thought—if anything happened to you—what a waste for her ... you know...

Paige Oh, I see. All the same, taking his favourite motor. You don't half believe in going out in style, do you?

Micky I won't keep it. I'll dump it. Coming with us?

Paige You're safer on your own, Micky. We both are.

Micky Sure?

Paige Separate ways.

Arabella I'll tell you what, we could stop for a drink, couldn't we? I know this gorgeous pub.

Micky I don't drink.

Arabella Oh, pity.

Micky It's got a musical cocktail cabinet in the back, though.

Arabella You need say no more, dear man.

Justin returns to use the phone

Justin ...I'll try this lot. I used them once before, they should be——— (*He sees Arabella and Micky at the door*) What's going on?

Arabella Justin, darling, this gentleman—this champion boxer—has kindly offered to drive me home.

Justin Has he?

Arabella It's apparently, so he says, on his way.

Justin I see.

Arabella (*kissing him*) So save your money, darling. And see you very soon, I hope.

Justin Yes, I hope so. 'Night.

Arabella 'Nighty-night.

Micky 'Bye. (*To Paige*) Sure?

Paige Positive.

Micky tosses her the front-door key and goes with Arabella

Micky! Thank you. Cheers, mate. Good luck.

Micky and Arabella exit

A pause

Justin So. You're free.

Paige For the time being. I'd better get moving as well. I can still get a tube to Hounslow. It's not that late. If you could lend me a little? You said you would. Just for the fare.

Justin Of course. (*He produces his wallet*) Here. (*He thrusts a fistful of notes at her*)

Paige looks doubtful

Please. Take it...

Paige I don't need all that. (*She hesitates*) I mean, I didn't even give you my full dance routine, did I? (*She takes the money*) Thanks. You're a very nice person.

Justin Thank you.

Paige For a man. No, true. Most men I know, if you look in their eyes, all you see is this hate. Incredible. They really hate us women, most of them. I've never known why that is. But I'm always seeing it. I mean, real, real hatred, you know. It's like we threaten them. And the more they love us, the more they need us—and the more they need us—the more they hate us because they need us. Bloody men. Crazy bastards.

Justin Do you see hatred in my eyes, then?

Paige (*examining him*) Nah.

Justin What do you see?

Paige Fear. Just fear.

Pause. Then before the moment can develop further she kisses him and presses the door key into his hand

(*Moving to the front door*) Thank you, Justin. Won't forget you. Have a good life, love. 'Bye.

Justin (*anxious to detain her a moment longer*) Paige?

Paige (*patiently*) What?

Justin That story of you and the motorbike and the nurse? Learning all over again? Was that true?

Paige (*after a beat*) No, I made it up. Just making conversation, that's all. 'Bye.

Justin (*stopping her again*) Look, take that coat there. The mac, it's mine.

Paige This one?

Justin At least you'll be warm.

Paige Ta. See you. (*She is about to open the door*)

Justin (*suddenly*) Paige!

Paige (*angrily*) What, Justin? What is it?

Justin (*softly*) Help me, please. Help me.

Paige What are you talking about?

Justin Help me. Take me with you.
Paige (*incredulously*) *What?*
Justin I'm begging you.
Paige You're mad.
Justin I feel I'm trapped here. I need to get away—I have to escape.
Paige Then get away. There's nothing to stop you.
Justin I don't have the courage. Not on my own.
Paige Justin. You don't know what you're asking, love.
Justin I know exactly what I'm asking.
Paige You come with me, you give up this flat—you give up your job—you
say goodbye to your girlfriend, all your friends, everything...
Justin I don't care.
Paige I couldn't do that to you, Justin. You're too nice a bloke. You can do
better than me, love.
Justin I don't think I can.

She looks at him

Please.

Pause

(*Imploringly*) Please.
Paige There'll be no looking back?
Justin No.
Paige No regrets later? Recriminations?
Justin Never.

Paige shakes her head in disbelief

Paige (*expressionless*) You're barking. (*After a beat*) Come on then, you sad
bastard, we'd better get moving then, hadn't we? (*She holds out her hand
to him*)

Justin moves to her. She kisses him briefly and they start out of the front door

Justin (*going, triumphantly*) *Yes!*
Paige (*going*) My God, this is *mad!*
Justin (*triumphantly*) *Yes!*

They exit. The door closes behind them

Dee, after a second, comes out of the bedroom

Dee (*calling back*) That's funny, there's nobody here.

Derek (*off, muffled*) Hotle her haying?

Dee (*calling*) What did you say, dear?

Derek (*off, muffled*) Harsing hot hoo haying?

Dee (*calling*) Can't hear you at all, dear.

Derek comes on

Derek Sorry, I can't hear you, dear.

Dee I'm saying there's no-one here.

Derek Well, he must have popped out.

Dee Yes.

Derek Probably seeing his mother off.

Dee She'll need some seeing off.

Derek She will.

Dee Those neighbours must have gone back upstairs.

Derek Good riddance.

Dee So say all of us.

Derek People like that. Not fit to be in a decent home. Rude. Bad language. Bad manners. I'd lock them up. I would. Throw away the key.

Dee You'd do right. How's our little Apple, then?

Derek I looked in just now. She's sleeping. Sleeping like a baby.

Dee Ah!

Derek Little fists clenched round her face, you know, like when she was little.

Dee Ah. Let's have a peep, shall we?

Derek Very quietly now. Don't wake her.

Dee Ever so quietly.

They tiptoe into the bedroom

The doorbell rings. Pause. The doorbell rings again. Pause. The doorbell rings a third time

Derek and Dee enter

It was. It was the doorbell. I'm sure it was.

A banging on the door. As of someone with a huge fist

Derek Oh, for goodness sake!

Dee They'll wake little Apple.

Derek Some people! There's no call for that.

The banging continues, getting louder

Dee See who it is, dear.

Derek I fully intend to. And furthermore I'll give them a piece of my mind. (*He moves to the door*)

Dee You do that.

Derek (*indignantly, opening the door*) Now listen, I don't know what you're playing at but I'm giving you fair warning that I intend to—— (*He opens the door and catches sight of whoever it is on the other side*)

A gloved hand of someone very tall grips the top of the door preventing Derek from closing it again. This is all we can see

(*Very alarmed*) Oh, dear God! Who are you?

Before we see the outcome, a rapid fade to Black-out

CURTAIN

FURNITURE AND PROPERTY LIST

Further dressing may be added at the director's discretion

ACT I

SCENE 1

On stage: Well-stocked bar with drinks and glasses
Desk
Chair
Sofa
Armchair
Heavy coffee table
Healthy pot plants
Small table
2 chairs
6 linen table napkins
Large tray
Cutlery in drawer
Serving spoons and forks
Cloth
Clock
Handbag containing car keys
Coats on pegs
CD player
CDs
Phone

Off stage: Empty tray (**Julie-Ann**)
5 dessert forks (**Julie-Ann**)
Large bath towel, blanket (**Justin**)
Fork (**Julie-Ann**)

Personal: **Micky:** gun in holster, keys on ring, wrist-watch (worn throughout)

SCENE 2

Set: Saucepan of soup heating on stove
            2 bottles of good white wine in fridge
            Corkscrew

Personal: **Micky:** front door mortice key

ACT II

Set: Bowl in sink filled with soapy water
            Dustpan and brush under sink
            Dessert fork under cushions

Off stage: Cup of coffee (**Julie-Ann**)
            Nearly-empty coffee cup (**Derek**)
            Empty glass (**Arabella**)
            Dirty plates and cutlery (**Justin** and **Women**)
            Cruets, mats, etc. (**Dee**)
            Kitchen chairs (**Julie-Ann**)

Personal: **Micky:** mobile phone
            Justin: wallet containing fistful of notes

LIGHTING PLOT

Property fittings required: nil
1 interior. The same throughout

ACT I, SCENE 1

To open: Evening lighting, stormy effects outside

Cue 1   **Micky**: "Anything we can do to help, then?"   (Page 25)
          Fade lights to black-out

ACT I, SCENE 2

To open: Evening lighting, stormy effects outside

Cue 2   **Justin** returns to the kitchen   (Page 37)
          Fade lights to black-out

ACT II

To open: Evening lighting

Cue 3   **Derek**: "Who are you?"   (Page 65)
          Rapidly fade lights to black-out

EFFECTS PLOT

ACT I

Cue 1	To open Scene 1 *Heavy rain and wind effects at windows, continuing*	(Page 1)
Cue 2	**Julie-Ann**: "...the state of the cutlery." *Fresh gust of wind and rain at window*	(Page 6)
Cue 3	**Justin** stands frowning *Phone rings*	(Page 8)
Cue 4	**Justin**: "...twelve bloody weeks. Oh, God..." *Phone rings*	(Page 13)
Cue 5	**Justin**: "What's there to live for...?" *Woman's long-drawn-out scream as if falling from some height outside*	(Page 13)
Cue 6	**Justin** opens a door *Increase storm effect, reduce when window closed*	(Page 14)
Cue 7	**Paige** and **Justin** go off *After brief pause, sound of bath running off*	(Page 18)
Cue 8	**Julie-Ann** exits and **Justin** sighs *Phone rings*	(Page 19)
Cue 9	**Justin** exits to dining-room *After pause, doorbell rings*	(Page 20)
Cue 10	**Justin** exits *Doorbell rings*	(Page 20)
Cue 11	**Micky** opens windows *Increase wind and rain effect*	(Page 20)

ACT II